The Cancer Guide

How to Nurture Wellbeing
Through and Beyond a
Cancer Diagnosis

The Cancer Guide

How to Nurture Wellbeing Through and Beyond a Cancer Diagnosis

PROFESSOR ANNE-MARIE O'DWYER

Bedford Square Publishers

First published in the UK in 2024 by Bedford Square Publishers Ltd,
London, UK

bedfordsquarepublishers.co.uk
@bedsqpublishers

A CIP catalogue record for this book is
available from the British Library.

ISBN
978-1-915798-28-2 (Trade Paperback)
978-1-915798-29-9 (eBook)

2 4 6 8 10 9 7 5 3 1

Typeset by Palimpsest Book Production Ltd, Falkirk, Stirlingshire

Printed and bound in Great Britain by CPI Group (UK) Ltd,
Croydon, CR0 4YY

CONTENTS

Prologue – A Letter to the Reader

Dear Reader,

If you have taken this book to read, it is likely you, or someone you care about, have been told they have, or may have, cancer. This book is for you – those who fear they may have cancer, those who already have cancer, those who have been treated for cancer – and your families, friends or clinicians.

Throughout, you will hear the phrase 'information is power'. During their cancer care, patients consistently said to me, 'If I had only known beforehand, it might not have been so difficult.' Knowing in advance what to expect helps you to prepare for or, even better, avoid, some of the difficulties associated with cancer and its treatment. The information must, however, be appropriate for you, your cancer and your treatment. In an age of information overload, misinformation is everywhere, potentially worsening, rather than helping, your situation.

I have written this book following almost four decades of clinical experience, more than half of which I have spent working directly with patients who have cancer.

As a consultant physician-psychiatrist with a focus on, and training in, psychological aspects of care, I have written this text about the human aspects of cancer. Human reactions to a cancer diagnosis – fear, terror, isolation, abandonment, courage, hope, tenacity, persistence – largely remain unchanged. They shape your experience of cancer and its treatment. The text presents stories, experiences and strategies that patients and clinicians shared during my clinical years – what they found helpful in managing cancer and their treatments. In many cases, patients specifically asked for their experiences to be passed on to help others.

Cancer never affects just one individual. It inevitably also affects families, loved ones, friends. *The Cancer Guide* provides specific information for family and friends. More broadly, I also hope that, by providing a window into the experiences of our patients – the thoughts, feelings and emotions they experience, often too difficult for them to share directly with you – this book will help you to better understand what is happening to them, guiding you to know how best to help.

Having worked with patients with cancer for many years, what has often been most impressive, in truth sometimes overwhelming, has been the determination, resilience, hope and kindness of our patients – in the most difficult of circumstances. This book shares some of these memorable stories – not of supermen (or -women) but extraordinary people, struggling to manage a difficult diagnosis, determined to make the best life within that. Their wisdom lives on in their stories, experiences and strategies.

I truly hope this book will inspire you, as patients and colleagues have, so often, inspired me.

Professor Anne-Marie O'Dwyer

PLEASE NOTE: All patient stories have been anonymised, sometimes combined, and amended to ensure no link to specific individuals.

Introduction – Cancer in Context

There are many myths that still exist about cancer. These myths drive people's fears, making the struggle with cancer even more difficult. Thankfully, almost everyone now recognises that many people with cancer recover, and recover fully. Survival rates and treatments are improving all the time. It is also important to remember that there are many different types of cancer. Even in the 'same' area – for example, lung cancer – there are different types. So, one can never compare oneself to someone else's 'cancer story'.

However, even people who 'know' this, when they hear the word 'cancer', feel frozen, terrified, distressed – unable to process clearly what is happening.

This book seeks to help those affected by cancer (patients, families and friends). It follows the path often taken by a patient with cancer – diagnosis, treatment and beyond. It aims to overturn myths and to identify the fears and worries that cancer brings. Psychological work in general (and this book in particular) is about finding ways to analyse these fears and worries and to find practical solutions – objectively and empathically. There is always a way.

Section I

A CANCER DIAGNOSIS

1

Before Diagnosis – the Worry of Cancer

The fear 'it might be cancer'

It was two days before Christmas when Ellen found the lump in her breast. Stressed, busy with her three children, her job, her home and her husband, she did not want to believe it at first. It couldn't be happening to her. She did not have time for this. Surely it was a mistake? A bruise? A bump she hadn't noticed?

At the back of her mind, however, the fear had started. She had seen her own mother die from breast cancer. Ellen tried to put it out of her mind. She argued with herself. She rediscovered her religion, bargained with God. She blocked it out – and waited.

But, over the next six months, awake and distressed most nights, the fear took over. She imagined the worst. Images of her mother's illness flooded her mind every time she closed her eyes. She imagined the devastation for her young children, images of her coffin being lowered into the ground, her children sobbing at the graveside… She couldn't inflict this on them – this wasn't a good time. They were all busy with school, exams, plans… She would leave it for now. Maybe it was nothing.

For six months, constant thoughts and images went around her head. Was it something she had done? Was it her fault? How would her children, her family manage? She told no one. She couldn't eat. She lost weight. This frightened her even more. The lump was still there. In fact, she thought it might be bigger. Every day she checked, hoping it was a bad dream.

Finally, one day, a concerned friend asked her what was wrong. Ellen broke down in tears and told her about her fears. Her friend acted immediately. Her family rallied round her and she started the journey of investigation.

Ellen's story will be familiar to many of you. The fear of getting cancer remains widespread. This may be due to personal experience – perhaps a family member or close friend died from cancer – or a 'cancer story' in the media. These experiences can hugely influence your understanding, and therefore your experience, of cancer. Unfortunately, while some of these fears and beliefs may be true, **many are not**. Yet these beliefs are responsible for the distress that people feel, the type of torment that Ellen's story describes.

This section discusses thoughts and responses of those who fear **they may have cancer**, the implications of those worries and how to manage them.

The fear of cancer – what is it?

The word 'cancer' still strikes fear into many people's hearts. Some people will not even say the word 'cancer'. What lies behind that fear varies, but there are some common themes.

Fear of suffering, pain, death and dying

Most people who 'find something' that suggests cancer automatically imagine the worst – suffering, pain, death and dying. This is particularly the case if they have had personal experience of someone close to them who has suffered in this way. They immediately imagine unbearable suffering and pain. They imagine dying in circumstances in which they have no control, untreated pain and unmanageable distress. Often, in addition to these thoughts, they will have images in their mind that have an even more powerful and distressing effect. The more one tries to block out these experiences, the stronger they become. People visualise them 'in their head', unable to see any alternatives.

Fear of distressing family and loved ones

Often when one looks at it more closely, it is the pain that people believe they will inflict on others, especially close **family** and **friends**, that distresses them most. Like Ellen, they imagine their children distraught at their graveside; they see coffins being lowered into the grave. They imagine their partners struggling to manage alone. They see elderly parents, distressed and bewildered at the premature death of one of their beloved children. Even considering having investigations causes them distress as they imagine the impact of the uncertainty and fear on their family.

Fear of loss

For many, the word cancer automatically implies **loss** – not just loss of life but loss of role, loss of power, loss of dignity, loss of independence, loss of the chance to watch their children move through life, to see their first day at school, at university, to meet their partner, to see their grandchildren. These are devastating thoughts and fears.

Fear of uncertainty

Many people describe the possibility of having cancer like having 'the rug pulled out from under them'. They say it is like watching their entire lives being thrown up in the air and waiting for the pieces to fall to see where they land. They do not want to consider this could happen to them.

Fear of vulnerability, lack of privacy

Many people are very private individuals. They do not want others to know of their vulnerability. Many say how they do not want the 'pity' of others.

These fears of cancer – why do they matter?

The thoughts and images described above as part of the 'fear of cancer' are extremely distressing. Anyone, with or without cancer, who thought these thoughts or had these images would be very distressed. Yet the person we are discussing at present **does not yet know if they actually have cancer**. They have noticed a lump or a persistent pain, or just 'don't feel right'. They are **concerned that they may have cancer**. So it is not cancer at present that is causing their distress, but the fear that they may have it – the thoughts, beliefs, behaviours – how they respond to the idea they may have cancer.

There are, of course, many different ways that people attempt to deal with their distress about possible cancer. Some of these, while understandable, can be very **unhelpful**.

Denial

Many of us use the psychological response of denial. When faced with overwhelming news, we often initially cannot process it fully – we literally cannot accept or believe it. 'Blocking it out' allows us to function. It allows us to gather our strength, identify our resources and work out how to manage and face the overwhelming situation presented to us. Often, people move in and out of denial or combine denial with reality. For them, it is a multilayered strategy. We have seen people faced with a life-threatening illness simultaneously book a holiday and write their will. They do not want to discuss their fear of death. They want to retain hope. Many people use denial (or partial denial) to help them cope, to help them continue with their lives. Denial (or partial denial) can, therefore, be helpful.

However, denial can also be very harmful, particularly when it prevents you from accessing help and treatment. Denial, at the very least, usually means delay in responding to what is happening. And, with cancer, usually it is better to establish early if it is there, so that treatment can be started early. Denial also prevents you from getting real facts about what is happening to you. Often people's fears are based on misinformation, or outdated information. Denial prevents you from acting to identify this. Imagine suffering six months of horrific distress, fearing you have cancer – only to find you do not have cancer at all.

Avoidance and deferral

These responses are very closely connected to denial. As in Ellen's story, people often recognise that they may **possibly** have cancer, but they will just **wait** to deal with it until… their son has finished his training; their daughter has started her first job; their husband has retired. Or they just avoid thinking about it, if possible, like Ellen, endlessly arguing with themselves in their head. *'It's not really there; I am imagining it – it's nothing'*, or busying themselves with other activities to block it out.

Unlike complete denial, in these cases people are unable to completely 'block it out' and continue to have the worries circulating around their head – a very distressing situation. Like denial, this causes delay in accessing care, again potentially adversely affecting their chance of cure.

Worry

Most people fearing they may have cancer will, inevitably, worry. They worry about the consequences of having cancer;

how they will manage treatment; what will happen to them, their family, their work. Sometimes the worry itself can spiral out of control, causing more distress, impairing the ability to think clearly, make reasoned judgements.

The fear of cancer – possible outcomes

If you have found something worrying, there really are only two scenarios:

You do not have cancer

There is no doubt that fear that one may have cancer can be terrifying and overwhelming. However, you may not have cancer – the distress, worry and fear you feel at present may be entirely unwarranted. There is a chance that you do not have cancer at all, that there is some other cause for your symptoms. Denial and avoidance are simply prolonging your distress and delaying your discovery that it is, in fact, a false alarm.

You do have cancer

While this statement may strike fear into your heart, it is an outcome that must be considered, but please be aware that many of the images and fears discussed above are driven by your unique view of cancer. This is, in turn, influenced by your experiences and beliefs. Many patients can describe in detail (and see in their mind) the cancer experience (and deaths) of close family relatives from years previously. Or they have seen dramatic portrayal of cancer diagnoses on TV or social media. Others are influenced by 'cancer myths' – universally accepted, misleading and unhelpful beliefs about cancer. Many of these fears are misplaced and untrue, yet exert a very powerful influence, often unconsciously.

The reality is that many cancers now are highly treatable. Many treatments have become much less toxic and much more successful. These thoughts, images and fears that drive so much distress, they are simply that – thoughts, images and fears. Thoughts, while they are very real to you, are not facts.

The fear of cancer – what to do next

Act

If you have noticed a lump, bump, bruise or pain, and worry you may have cancer, act, and act as soon as you can. Yes, this will require you to acknowledge that there is a chance you may have cancer (a frightening prospect), but consider the options. Some of your fear may be driven by misinformation. Delay is potentially worsening your outcome. If 'in denial', you can use it, initially, to help you to gather yourself, to consider your options. You may even decide to continue to use 'partial denial' throughout your treatment. But do not allow it to trap you into complete inaction. Instead of helping you, denial can then become a very harmful strategy. Get help from others. Visit your family doctor (GP) and tell your story. Be aware that some of your friends and family may already suspect there is something bothering you and are just waiting for a chance to help you. Identify people you trust and who can support you. Bring someone you trust with you to your appointment.

If you find you do not have cancer – a wonderful outcome – then put this book aside. If you find you do have cancer, the rest of this book presents information from people who found themselves in that position, and found ways to live their lives despite that.

I hope it will help.

2

Cancer – Seeking a Diagnosis – the 'Tunnel of Tests'

Anne finally plucked up the courage to visit her GP. She hadn't told anyone in her family about the constant pain and swelling in her tummy, hoping that if she didn't discuss it, it wouldn't be real. But it was now too bad to ignore. She had finally booked an appointment with Dr Ryan, a kind man, and her family doctor for more than 20 years.

Haltingly, she told her story, carefully watching the doctor's face for any sign of alarm. She watched him closely again as he examined her tummy – noticing that he seemed to spend a long time feeling in one area. 'Was that it?' she thought. 'Had he found a cancer?' He told her that she was wise to attend, that he could not tell what the problem was, but that he would like to order tests – bloods, X-rays, scans – and refer her for another opinion. Anne's fear increased, her hopes that he would tell her it was 'fine, nothing to worry about' dashed. She could hardly hear what he was saying. Mutely, she took the list of tests and headed to the nurse's office for her blood tests.

The following weeks passed in a blur. She had to have X-rays, scans, more scans. Every time her phone rang, she jumped, fearing the worst. Every test she had, she scrutinised the face of the examiner, certain she could read the answer in their face, or their replies. It was a rollercoaster of emotions.

Finally, here she was, at the gynaecologist's office, waiting to be seen, to be told the results. Exhausted from lack of sleep, overwhelmed by fear, she did not even hear her name being called. Her sister took her by the hand. Gratefully she accepted her help. She did not think she could hear the news alone.

Seeking a diagnosis, the 'tunnel of tests'

What is the 'tunnel of tests'?

We are sometimes asked to see patients at this stage of their cancer 'journey'. Fearful they may have cancer, but not yet sure of their diagnosis, they embark on a 'conveyor belt' of tests – usually multiple types of investigations, in multiple sites, from multiple people. Why do we call this the 'tunnel of tests'? Because, based on our experience with patients at this point, that is what best describes it. People must go through this tunnel, to the light at the far side, to discover the answer to their question – *Do I have cancer?* And while it can be, for many, absolutely terrifying, it is a journey they must undertake to get the correct help. It is like taking a deep breath to swim underwater to get to an exit. Intensive psychological intervention, input, work is very unlikely to help in the short time available. Sometimes, for overwhelming anxiety, or severe insomnia, or fear that prevents them being in a scanner, patients may need short-term medication. This can usually be prescribed by their family doctor or their consultant. Generally, though, patients must get through that tunnel, supported by family and friends, to get to the far side, where they will get an answer, and, even more importantly, a plan of action.

The 'conveyor belt' experience

This 'conveyor belt' is the reality of modern-day medicine. Any potential cancer diagnosis is (appropriately) investigated from multiple different perspectives. Even when the results are back, frequently they are discussed and reviewed by a team of specialists, the 'multidisciplinary team' (MDT), to ensure patients benefit from multiple viewpoints of expertise, before any clear diagnosis or plan can be made.

While this is necessary to ensure best care, it can be very distressing for patients. Every test that they have, patients expect will show the answer. Like Anne, every test they watch carefully and ruminate on the process, searching for a clue, any clue that they may, or may not, have cancer. Yet the reality is many of the people carrying out the tests do not have the answer. They often do not even have access to the results. They are carrying out the procedure. Even if they did have an answer for their single test, as described above, **it is the combination of tests and investigations that is now used to make a diagnosis and plan**. The reality is that much of this worry and guesswork is worsening your experience – for no real gain.

This, then, can be an extremely difficult time for you. Recurrently, patients have told us that it is the **uncertainty** during this time that is most difficult. They feel like they are 'waiting for the axe to fall', without any plan in place to deal with it. They cannot help but try to interpret words, glances, phrases. When they look back, they wish someone had told them what we have said above – that no one test is the answer, that the looks/phrases/expressions were usually not loaded with meaning. They were likely influenced by something else entirely, not to do with them at all. So, while it is an extremely difficult process, and is like a cage you long to escape from immediately, it is a process you cannot hurry, nor 'guess' the end result. It is a tunnel you must go through – a distressing, fear-inducing, horrible experience, but one that is necessary to provide you with the best answer and best plan for your query.

As always, however, there are some things that you can do, or not do, that can help you as you go through that 'tunnel'.

Share your fears

Share your fears. This will be a recurrent theme throughout this book. So often, we hear from patients that they did not want to 'upset' their loved ones by telling them how distressed and afraid they were, and how the hardest thing was hiding that from them. We then hear, from the same relatives, how distressed and afraid they are for their loved one who is sick, and how the hardest thing is hiding that from them. This leads to a double burden. Both are not only experiencing extra distress from the strain and tension of concealment from each other, they are also losing out on the opportunity to get help, to benefit from support. Your personal support network will be one of the most important things you have during this time. Think carefully about who is most important to you and who is most likely to help. Then decide how much you feel able to share. Concealment is rarely the right approach.

Dr Google – a potentially unhelpful friend

Brendan, a young married father of three very young children, had extensive treatment for cancer over a six-month period. Within a year it had returned. His treatment options were limited. He was distraught, overwhelmed. Thoughts of not being there for his young children were torturing him. He felt he had already missed six months of their lives having his treatment the previous year. He was unable to sleep, eat, rest, engage with his children or his wife. Reluctantly, he attended psycho-oncology, saying to me, 'What can you do? This is not "in my head". I don't need a psychiatrist. I have looked it up on Google – I check every day. My options are terrible. I will be dead in a year'.

As he sat opposite me in my out-patients, my heart sank. So much of what Brendan said was true. He was a young man, a father of three young children, and his treatment options were limited. Google was confirming his worst fears, and his distress was preventing him from engaging with the time he had now. To use the time he had now, precious time, he would need to move away from confirming his worst fears on Google. But first, I had to find a way to engage him. I could also sense his fear, desolation and distress, his conviction that no one could bear this either. I knew that the next few minutes of conversation would be crucial.

I paused to reflect on what he had said. Brendan had told me that he owned and managed a small stud farm. Aware that he was completely focused on the terrible prognosis and advice offered by the internet, and knowing that he would not be able to engage with any psychological intervention unless that preoccupation could be shaken, I again asked him about Google and if he thought the internet was a reliable source of information.

'Absolutely,' he said. 'I search the most reliable sites.'

'That is great,' I replied, 'because I am thinking of leaving my job and would love to start a stud farm, so I look forward to using Google to help me to do that.'

'Ah, but that's different,' said Brendan. 'That is a very complex thing, selecting the right horses. You can't use Google for that. You would need to get specialist advice, specifically for you, for that.' There was a pause while Brendan took in what he had just said. 'Okay,' he said, 'talk on – I will listen.'

As Brendan was leaving our building that morning, he said to our Clinical Nurse Specialist, who had helped with his assessment, 'She's a tough one. Didn't flinch at any of it. I will give the plan a go.'

Brendan shifted from searching the internet for hours every evening, to focusing on every minute he had with his family, at that moment. Two months later, in a phone-call review (asked for as he did not want to waste any time commuting), Brendan was out mending fences on his land with his three young boys.

'I am using what time I have now', he said, 'every moment is precious'.

In the modern age of ready access to information, we have all become accustomed to 'googling' the answer to almost everything. It is extremely difficult to ask people not to google for information. Patients often regard us with suspicion – asking what are we trying to hide. But the reality is, information on the internet is not tailored to the individual person. This is particularly so when people have multiple symptoms that may or may not indicate cancer. People are correct when they say, 'information is power' – but only when it is the right information for them. Yes, it is extremely difficult to wait. But, until all the tests are complete, and reviewed, and interpreted by those best placed to understand them, the correct answer will not be available. To use a very mundane example – if you were standing on a platform waiting for a train to a specific destination, you would not just hop on a train that pulled in because you were finding the waiting too difficult – **you would wait for the train going to the correct destination.** So, while it is excruciatingly difficult, 'waiting for the **correct** answer', rather than searching for unstructured information on Google, is likely to be the better option.

Identify your support network

For some people, waiting to hear is just intolerable. It increases their sense of distress and vulnerability, their sense of powerlessness. What you can do during this uncertain period is begin to look at your own support networks – those that are close to you; those whom you trust; those that are dependable; those that could help with practical tasks if you need it. Have a scheme for your network of support that you can activate if needed at the end of your investigations.

The exit from the 'tunnel of tests' – having an answer, having a plan

As we have said, recurrently, patients have told us that what is particularly terrifying during this time of multiple tests is not knowing what the answer will be, and not having a **plan of action** to focus on. Often they suspect they may have cancer. And their fears may be confirmed. But what has been particularly terrifying is the feeling that no one has a plan for them. One of the benefits of waiting for the final integration of tests is that the diagnosis will (usually) then be delivered **with the correct plan** for them. It is the certainty of a way forward, a plan, that patients describe as the most helpful end to this first stage. First, however, you must hear the results.

Hearing the results

No matter how well one prepares, hearing one has a diagnosis of cancer is never easy, and for many, remains terrifying. It is crucially important to bring someone with you for this visit. Many people stop hearing what is being said after the first sentence, the first time cancer is mentioned. You may have heard snatches of information, facts or figures, but often you will be unable to process it. Bringing someone you trust with you is crucial. They can absorb the information on your behalf, even write it down for you, and go over it with you later. They can help you to focus on a plan for a way forward, once you have gathered yourself from the shock of hearing you have cancer. They can also repeat the information your consultant has given you, ensuring you do not resort to 'Dr Google' for your information.

You have cancer. Yes, that is difficult. But now, the question is, how to go on living with that diagnosis. That may seem too hard to consider at present. But that is where you must go next – living with, despite, the diagnosis.

3

Cancer – Receiving a Diagnosis – 'Picking up the Pieces'

There is no single way that people respond to a diagnosis of cancer. Some people describe 'putting off' thinking about it, focusing instead on getting through their treatment without really considering the impact of their diagnosis of cancer until later. Others are immediately 'hit' by the impact. Still others are somewhere in between – fluctuating between acting as if nothing is happening and intermittently being overwhelmed. Some simply accept it as a fact of life, focus on treatment and move on, adapting the 'tunnel of tests' approach for a 'tunnel of treatment'. Thus, in presenting possible reactions, we recognise that there is no 'one-size-fits-all' response. Neither is there one 'best way' to manage it. This text presents the range of experiences people have described and the strategies they found helpful in managing these.

There is, of course, much overlap between all these emotions – fear, distress, grief are all interlinked. They are separated here partly because some people experience each differently, and to help give structure to a plan to tackle and manage them.

Much like the 'tunnel of tests', often when people are in treatment, particularly starting treatment, they can find it very difficult to concentrate on any psychological work. Sometimes, therefore, simply hearing that what you are experiencing is 'normal', 'typical' for someone at this stage of their cancer journey can be enough to help you to settle.

We have given examples of the most common experiences people have below, together with some simple strategies.

Initial reactions to a diagnosis of cancer

Fear and distress

The commonest feeling that people describe on hearing they have cancer is fear – ranging from mild anxiety to over-whelming terror. The response is usually determined by their prior experiences or beliefs and therefore may not necessarily reflect the **reality** of what they have been told. Furthermore, they may not even have properly heard what they have been told.

What do people fear?

People's fears are usually like those they had when they found a 'warning sign' – worsened now by finding this is a reality. People fear death, or often, more specifically, they fear a slow or painful death. People fear the (psychological) pain they will inflict on others. They imagine the distress of their children, their partners, their parents, their friends. They fear the financial hardships their diagnosis will bring, the disruption to their lives and the lives of their families. Sometimes, they cannot describe exactly what it is they fear, describing instead an automatic response to the word cancer, 'something visceral' that is deep-rooted. They find themselves shaking, trembling, their thoughts caught in an endless loop of disaster scenarios, sometimes vivid images of these scenarios. They describe sobbing, crying for endless periods, seemingly unable to stop.

What are the effects of this fear?

While small amounts of anxiety can be helpful, often motivating us to do things we would rather put off, significant fear is crippling. It takes over, freezing people into inactivity. People describe being unable to think, unable to plan. Even though, for them, they may be physically well at present, they are unable to focus on the present, to function in the present, because of the 'fog' of fear that has invaded their lives.

What to do about this fear?

If you read the last paragraph carefully, you will see what is a central concept in this book. This concept, that our emotional reaction to cancer can distort our reality so that it can invade even our 'healthy' lives, is a theme you will see repeated throughout this book. Tackling this distortion (if present) is one of the most important tools people can use in their goal to manage a cancer diagnosis.

As has been suggested already, people's fear of cancer is influenced by many things – prior experience, personal history – many of which represent misinformation. This misinformation, particularly when kept hidden, **a silent fear**, can be very powerful. People are often afraid to voice it – somehow that will make it real.

In doing psychological work within a medical setting (in cancer, called psycho-oncology), we are constantly looking to change the parts we can change, the parts that are under our control. While cancer will undoubtedly affect your lives, what we want to do is keep that effect to the 'least amount possible'. Much like the 'tunnel of tests', often when people are in treatment, particularly starting treatment, they can find it very difficult to concentrate on any psychological work. If you can, make a list of what exactly you fear – and on what you have based this fear. Bring the information with you to your cancer team. You are likely to find that much of the information and experience you have listed is not relevant to your situation.

Grief and loss

Loss is one of the key impacts of a cancer diagnosis, and **grief** a central emotional response to loss. The (potential) losses associated with cancer are many. Loss of life is clearly central, but there are many other feared losses – loss of function, loss of role, loss of independence. There is also loss of certainty – a feeling so many of us (mistakenly) take for granted, and only appreciate when we have lost it. People also describe fear of the loss of many opportunities and occasions – to see children advance through their lives, to help choose their schooling, to support families, parents, friends, to follow the dreams and plans they had.

Some of the losses are subtle, and difficult for family and friends to understand.

I was asked to see John, a 46-year-old married father of two, an in-patient waiting for cancer treatment. His nurse said he was utterly despondent, withdrawn, not interacting with anyone on the ward. Yet his cancer was curable. His cancer team were struggling to understand his utter sadness.

Initially, John did not want to speak. What he had to say, in his view, told too much about him, things he did not want to say. He was not someone who normally liked to talk. He took a while to share his story.

He knew he had cancer. He knew there was a good chance he could be cured. But he had found the whole process utterly humiliating – he felt 'stripped of his dignity'. A busy farmer, proud of his physical ability to manage a difficult farm, to provide for his family, he was now too weak to do even the most basic of tasks. He described his utter humiliation watching his young son head out to manage their herd of cows alone. This, he felt, was his role. He should be able to provide.

John's family, meanwhile, were utterly distraught by his diagnosis. A loving, generous husband, father, brother and son, who had worked throughout his life to help them all, they now desperately wanted to help him – but could not get through to him. Careful discussion with John identified several facts he could agree with. He agreed he had been a generous, loving, capable person for his family. He agreed that he had 'earned' their respect and love. Most importantly, he acknowledged that if someone else in his family was in his position, he would want to help them. In fact, he would have found it distressing, even humiliating, to be denied the chance to help. He smiled, ruefully, at that point, understanding the inconsistencies in what he was saying. A further step was acknowledging that this situation was temporary, that ultimately, he could go back to being the capable, responsible, loving, providing person he still was. He acknowledged that, in fact, the quickest way to do that was to delegate tasks he could not do, for now, to those people who most loved him and wanted to help, due, of course, to the care and love he had shown to them.

In John's case, for example, with an expected cure, his team and family found it hard to understand what was causing him such distress. Yet, to the person experiencing them, the 'subtle' losses, described by John, are often the most difficult to bear – even temporarily.

What are the effects of grief and loss?

As with fear, grief is an overwhelming, incapacitating emotion. It is also often deeply corrosive – people describe it as 'eating away at me'. Racked by sadness, overwhelmed by feelings of loss, people are unable to focus on the here and now, to avail themselves of what they have, connect with people close to them who want to help.

What to do about this grief?

Much like with distress, one of the key approaches is to first identify exactly what is happening – what is central to these feelings. What does your grief centre on? Too often, people who are trying to help, make assumptions about what is important for the person with cancer. This is a dangerous action. The damage then is twofold. Firstly, they cannot intervene successfully as they have not correctly identified the issue. Secondly, they lose that person's trust in their ability to help, potentially compounding the person's sense of loss and hopelessness ('not even their loved ones can help').

John's story shows the importance of careful **listening**, of initially defining the core problem and then examining the beliefs underlying this, to help them access the help they need and deserve.

John's story can be used as the template for each of the senses of loss described above – for you yourself to use, or for families or friends to use with you. When examined, it was John's sense of loss of role, loss of dignity, his sense of humiliation, that was incapacitating him – **not his cancer**. This was a loss that was temporary, understandable – but neither he nor his team had been able to identify it. Understanding this helped, not only John but also his family, who could then manage their distress on his behalf and support him in a practical way.

It is rarely easy to think clearly when distressed. You may need to identify one person in your family or friends with whom you can share your distress. They can then act on your behalf with others. Or you may need to identify someone on your cancer team to help you. Getting help to recognise what is driving your fears is a key first step in helping you to engage with your life. Because, to quote one of our patients, a central message that cancer gives to everyone who gets it is 'Every moment is precious and the time to use that moment is now.'

Other responses to a cancer diagnosis
and how to manage them

Of course, there are an infinite number of possible responses to cancer. The ones above are the most common, and usually the most persistent. A number of other responses are listed below.

Distortion of reality
People often describe a sense that everything is 'unreal' or 'distorted' when they hear their cancer diagnosis. They describe seeing others 'from a distance', watching in amazement as those people continue with their lives, as normal, while they feel completely disconnected and unable to take part. Everything seems pointless.

This feeling of unreality is usually present at the start of their diagnosis and is often fleeting.

Denial
We have already discussed denial. Partial denial can be helpful – it gives people time to gather themselves and make plans. I have had patients who alternate between cheerfully discussing holidays that we both know they cannot take and planning their rigorous cancer treatment for the following months. People often use this partial or fluctuating denial to help them to manage. And they do not want someone to take that from them. Absolute denial – being unable to accept or believe anything about their cancer is true – is rare. If present, it is very difficult for family and friends to manage. As with the other situations, it requires the ability to listen,

to withhold judgement and to find ways to support the person who is on a very difficult journey.

Anger and injustice

Many patients have a huge sense of anger and injustice at a diagnosis of cancer. 'Why me? What did I do to deserve this? It is ridiculous. It is unfair. It is unjust. I have lived a healthy life. I am a good person. It is just not fair.'

Cancer teaches us many things and, unfortunately, one of those is that life is not fair. Life can be very unjust and bad things happen to good people.

While anger is often entirely understandable, anger, like grief, can be a very corrosive and unhelpful emotion. In small amounts, and for short periods, it can be a great motivator, but ultimately it causes you to get 'stuck'. It is (generally) not helpful for you – and what is helpful for you is what you will need to focus on. One patient, after many weeks of feeling upset and angry, searching for the 'why' of her cancer and, in particular, 'why me', said, *'I woke up this morning and thought – okay, I finally get it. There is no answer, **no specific reason** why I got this cancer. The question is not "why me?", the question is "why not me?" Now, how can I move on?'*

Shame

Many people will be surprised to see the word 'shame' as a reaction to the worry of cancer. Yet many people describe feeling shamed, stigmatised by a diagnosis of cancer. They worry they have caused it themselves, that they will be judged by others. An unhelpful belief that 'stress' caused their cancer, for example, makes them doubt and judge themselves, thinking they are responsible for their plight. Others, much like John in the story above, feel shame as they see themselves as 'useless', unable to do the roles they previously did, watching as others must do the most basic tasks for them. Most people will accept, in discussion, that they would never knowingly have done anything to cause their cancer. Furthermore, they will usually readily acknowledge that they would not 'judge' others, and the concept that someone with cancer should carry the additional burden of shame will seem very unjust. Where shame is caused by a sense of feeling 'useless', using the strategies described in John's story – recognising that the need for help will be short-lived; that the quickest way to get better is to accept help when needed; that those around you will often be desperate to find ways to help you – and giving them a practical task helps not only you, but also them.

Isolation

In the early stages of a cancer diagnosis and treatment, patients can feel a huge sense of isolation. They feel as if they are the only person experiencing something as awful as this. The recurrent nausea and vomiting, the hair loss, the disfiguring effects of surgery, all combine to make them feel 'set apart', 'different'.

With time, however, and as they visit the cancer centre, they see many others grappling with the same issues. Many, many people have cancer, each struggling in their own way to manage it. Often, you just do not see them. Their treatment and distress are not visible. You are not alone.

For some, meeting and engaging with other people who have had (or have) cancer can be very helpful in managing the sense of isolation. For most, however, the most helpful route is to identify your own support network – not in the cancer setting – family and friends who will want to support you in getting through this and making it to the far side.

So...

You will have been given your cancer diagnosis and a plan for treatment and care. Initially, you will likely feel angry, shocked, distressed, afraid – unable to believe it. After the initial shock, most people find that they gather themselves to start out on the journey of dealing with cancer, taking whatever treatment is necessary. Often the focus and structure that this gives, the regular visits to the hospital, provide relief and distraction from the immediate distress. Some patients go through this phase of treatment 'with their eyes closed', making it to the end of their treatment, when they will start their lives again – a 'tunnel of treatment'. You may not have significant distress during this time – you are in a form of (helpful) denial and avoidance, doing what is needed to do to make it through. Sometimes, it is at the end of this journey, the end of treatment that the full impact becomes apparent. For others, you may need help to get through your treatment. Help is always available – personal, from family or friends; professional, from your cancer team or your own family doctor.

Section II

MOVING TO
CANCER TREATMENT –
A PSYCHO-ONCOLOGY
PERSPECTIVE

4

Knowing Your Cancer Treatment Team

There are a bewildering number of different treatments for cancer, and an equally bewildering number of treatment specialists. Once you move to receive treatment for cancer, you will be supported by a cancer team. This chapter gives you information about your team – the various people and team members you may encounter as part of your treatment. Many of their names and roles will be unfamiliar to you. This chapter aims to provide you with information and education about them in order to help you to manage your cancer. If you are not clear, ask someone on your team to point you in the right direction. You can also ask for information for your family and friends. It will help them to help you.

Your cancer-treating team

A good team is key to everything. Each person on a team provides a different skill, a different perspective, different expertise. Make sure to 'use' every person on your team. They will help you – individually and together. I have included a brief description of some possible members of your team below. Different areas in the world may have different config-urations and different teams – ask in your own cancer centre for information on who may be available to you if you are not certain. The descriptions of their roles are also brief – this reflects the fact some of these are not my areas of expertise, and that it is best for you to get the extra information by speaking to them yourself. This list is a 'starter', an introduction.

Cancer doctors – physicians, surgeons, radiation therapists

Many doctors train in the assessment and treatment of cancer. Each usually then specialises in specific areas – **Medical** Oncologist, delivery of 'medical' cancer care, for example chemotherapy; **Surgical** Oncologist, delivery of surgical treatment; **Radiation** Oncologist, delivery of radia-tion treatment. Some patients, for example with breast cancer, may be under the care of three specialities – surgery, chemo-therapy and radiation therapy. Others may only need one form of treatment, for example surgery. Quite often, you will be supervised and followed up over time by the medical oncologist, who will co-ordinate all your care. Often you will hear the team talking about 'reviewing your case at an MDT (multi-disciplinary) team meeting'. This means that your care will be reviewed, together, by several of these specialists (and others) to ensure you get the best care. Doctors often specialise further – for example by patient age (paediatric oncologist dealing with children) or by disease type – for example breast cancer; head and neck cancer. Usually, the cancer doctor directs and co-ordinates your care, planning your treatments and ensuring they are delivered.

Cancer nurses

The importance of the role of cancer nurses in your treatment cannot be overstated. Many patients with cancer describe them as 'the rock' to which they cling along their journey. The roles of cancer nurses are constantly developing, with an ever-increasing level of skills and responsibilities, including Clinical Nurse Specialists, Advanced Nurse Practitioners, skilled chemotherapy nurses and ward-based nurses, to name but a few. Whatever their title, nurses play a central role in any patient's experience. They are usually one of the first people you will meet, and many will become familiar faces to you, and a source of huge support, particularly if you are a regular attender at a cancer clinic. They provide a range of expertise including an understanding of both medical and psychological aspects of care. They are often the first person to notice any changes in your progress and will alert and co-ordinate with the team to set up the necessary changes.

Occupational therapy

Occupational therapists (OTs) support you in carrying out the activities of daily life. These can become overwhelming when you are faced with physical, psychological or social difficulties. OTs are expert in analysing every-day tasks, working out where the problems lie and working with you to generate practical solutions. This may include visiting your home with you to assess how your environment there can be improved to help you. Sometimes, this can involve making difficult decisions, adapting your home for a wheelchair, moving your bed out of your bedroom into the living area – decisions that make your illness real. It is very helpful to have a professional helping you and your family in making these difficult decisions, some of which may be temporary, all of which are focused on improving your quality of life now.

Physiotherapy

Physiotherapists will help you to maximise your **physical** abilities throughout your cancer care. Ideally, this will include meeting you before your treatments, especially surgery, to help prepare you for the physical impact of surgery, and advise you how to plan your recovery after surgery. Physiotherapists will advise you on how best to train your muscles to 'work' well again during and after prolonged bed rest, how to keep your lungs working well despite bed rest or surgery. Of course, nothing works in isolation, and while physiotherapists concentrate on physical wellbeing, invariably psychological factors come into play. Your physiotherapist, often working with other members of the team, will also help with the demoralisation and exhaustion that can happen, working with the Psycho-oncology service, for example, to support, encourage and motivate you in your recovery.

Medical social work

Medical social workers help patients and families to solve practical, financial, social and emotional difficulties. They look at how your illness may impact you and your family, liaise to help with your discharge home, including liaising with community services, and advocate on your behalf for resources that are needed.

Clinical nutrition

Having cancer treatments may cause problems with eating. This ranges from those patients who have had head and neck surgery, who may not be able to eat or drink at all, to those with nausea from chemotherapy drugs, to patients having a bone-marrow transplant, who face multiple problems, including ulceration of their mouth and gut, and fears of infection, which make them very hesitant about eating. This is further complicated by the fact that good nutrition, maintaining your physical strength and muscle mass, is key to recovery. Your clinical nutritionist (dietician) will advise you about your best options for diet, to help maximise your recovery. As always, this is often a complex task, taking account not only of physical but also psychological factors – so that working in a team is key.

Psycho-oncology

Psycho-oncology – the core of this book – refers to psychological aspects of cancer and its treatment. Every cancer carries a burden of a 'psychological' or 'human' impact, and no person is immune from a 'human' response. How individual people respond differs hugely – a sign of their individuality. Psychological factors play a role, not only in a person's distress and reaction to a cancer diagnosis, but also in their cancer treatment.

The role of psycho-oncology can include helping you to manage the impact of a cancer diagnosis, to manage the side-effects of treatment, or, to 'reclaim your life' after treatment. Sometimes, the role is simply to support you as you make your way through your cancer care. My own experience initially training in medical oncology highlighted for me the importance of psychological support for patients with cancer. It led me to move to psychological training and, later, to set up a Psycho-oncology Service at the hospital where I had first trained.

Psycho-oncology is still a relatively new speciality. However, many cancer services now have psycho-oncology teams, providing psychological assessment and interventions delivered by a team of experts in both mental health and cancer, including mental health nurses, clinical nurse specialists, advanced nurse practitioners, clinical psychologists and psychiatrists. Together these teams work with the cancer teams in assessing cancer needs, planning and delivering patient care, including psychological treatments.

Palliative care

The Palliative Care team is a key part of cancer care. Previously, it was seen as meaning 'end-of-life' care, but it is now firmly placed within the realm of cancer (and other illness) treatment at any stage of the pathway. Because of the nature of their work, their focus on managing symptoms rather than 'curing' disease, and their experience in providing end-of-life care, palliative care teams are comfortable in considering all aspects of patients' needs – physical, psychological and spiritual. They are expert, and more importantly, comfortable in talking to patients about subjects such as death and end-of-life care, subjects that are often extremely difficult, for everyone, in the setting of acute, high-intensity curative treatments. Ideally, palliative care is integrated within cancer care from the beginning, or, when needed, to manage challenging symptoms. For many patients, their relationship with their team is key. It is far better for them to have met and know their palliative care team early on in their care, rather than meeting them for the first time at the end of their care. The relationships made then make it much easier to engage with them in what is often a very difficult time, for patients and families.

Spiritual care

There are usually specific experts to support patients' spiritual and religious care needs in cancer. The impact of a cancer diagnosis and treatment often leads to changes in spiritual needs. Religious and spiritual leaders can provide the space and time to discuss these, often to include families as well as patients.

Cancer doctors – genetics

Cancer genetics is a relatively new field of cancer care – new specialities are developing all the time. While they may not be part of every cancer team, the role of cancer genetics has developed significantly in recent years. **Cancer genetics** teams specialise in identifying those cancers that are associated with 'genetic' abnormalities – changes to certain genes that control the way our cells divide and grow. In a small number (around 5%) of cancers, these genetic changes can be inherited within families. If your cancer doctor believes that this may apply to your cancer, they may refer you to a cancer genetics clinic to do genetic testing. These tests can then tell whether other family members, who have not yet developed cancer, also 'carry' these genetic changes, and may be at risk of developing cancer at a later stage. With this information, these family members may decide to have treatment to prevent the cancer from happening. An example of this is some forms of breast cancer. These are very difficult decisions, as this group will suffer many of the concerns and fears we are discussing in this book without having cancer themselves. They will also have to consider the impact of this diagnosis on their children, who may have inherited the gene. Some will struggle to manage this, feeling a sense of guilt and distress for 'passing on the gene'. Like many in this book, they will have to consider how to manage this, recognising that, while they **may** have passed on a gene for cancer to beloved children, clearly this was not done deliberately. Often these parents are going on to have major surgery, without cancer, to ensure they are doing everything possible to be there for their children and to support them.

Family and friends

Family and friends are usually an essential part of your cancer care and are discussed in a specific chapter later in the book. This chapter is focused on **professional team members**, who are generally not part of the family or friends circle.

Everyone else

Of course, the reality is that every person you encounter in the hospital plays a key role in your recovery – the porter, the cleaner, the caterer, to name but a few. This was bluntly described by the playwright and novelist Alan Bennett, who described his encounter with a hospital receptionist during his cancer care in the following (edited) quote: *'Listen… you are as essential to the work of this hospital as its most exalted consultant. You can do more for the spirits of patients coming to this institution than the most skilful surgeon… just by being nice.'* (Writing Home, p. 349). While Alan Bennett described what can happen when a person is less than helpful, many patients recount stories of the wonderful impact of small acts of kindness while attending the hospital – unprompted acts that people do that they do not have to do, people going beyond their role – making a signficant difference. In fact, it is one of the privileges for those of us working in health care. We have the chance to make a difference for our patients with small acts of kindness. Small random acts of kindness (stopping to acknowledge and talk to someone; bringing a cup of tea; finding a wheelchair), regularly done by health-care assistants, security staff, secretaries, catering staff, porters, doctors and nurses can make a real difference for patients' experience of cancer. I know, because I have seen them happen myself.

5

Cancer Treatments – Medical Oncology

Cancer treatments are constantly developing. The range of human psychological responses to cancer and its treatment remain relatively constant over time. Having information in advance about your treatment is important as it will help you to manage your anxieties. For more detailed information about your specific treatment, please ask your cancer team, read any booklets they give you, and/or ask your family to read them if you do not feel able. It is very helpful for your family to know what is happening. This allows them to help you and to be less afraid themselves about what is happening. This chapter focuses on the more common psychological problems that may arise during medical oncology care.

Overview of medical treatments (oncology/chemotherapy)

Almost all cancers have some form of 'medical' treatment (as distinct from surgery or radiotherapy). Previously, when one used the term 'medical treatments' this would largely mean 'chemotherapy'. With recent advances, this section now includes many new types of treatment. While this book is very firmly focused on psychological aspects of cancer care, brief descriptions of some of the medical treatments are given below, to help in explaining psychological responses.

Medical treatments include:

- **Chemotherapy** This refers to powerful 'cytotoxic' drugs that kill rapidly growing cells like cancer cells. It is used to treat and cure cancer, to prepare you for other cancer treatments (like bone-marrow transplantation), to reduce the size and effects of a cancer.
- **Immune therapy** (also called biological therapy) These treatments help your body's own defence (immune) systems to recognise and attack the cancer cells
- **Hormone therapy** Some cancers, particularly some types of breast and prostate cancers, are stimulated by hormones. Removing these hormones, or blocking them from acting, can stop the cancer from growing.
- **Targeted therapies** These are often a type of 'chemo-therapy' or drug therapy that 'target' (only bind to) a particular type of cancer cell and/or a particular function of that cell, for example they may disrupt cell signalling, cell function, or cell nutrition

This list is constantly growing and developing and is likely to change again over the next decade. This section focuses on the more common psychological issues that arise in the context of getting medical treatments for cancer. Some of these can happen whatever drug treatment is being given. Others are specific to the drug type. Always ask your doctor to explain what drug you are getting and the likely side-effects. This information will allow you to understand and manage what is happening.

Bone-marrow transplantation (BMT)

Bone-marrow transplantation (BMT) is a specific way of delivering 'medical treatment' for blood-related cancer. It means that your own 'starter' blood cells (cells found in the core of your bones that produce all your blood cells) must be killed off and you will be given new 'starter' cells. Although there is now a spectrum of BMT types, with some milder than others, it generally means that you must come into hospital for several days before the transplant to get high-dose chemotherapy to disable your own blood cells and prepare for the new ones. It is therefore a more complex treatment. Some of the effects are those of (very high-dose) chemotherapy. As it generally requires a prolonged hospital stay and long periods of isolation in a highly-controlled sterile environment to protect you from infection (the BMT unit), it can also have an impact beyond that of chemotherapy alone. Where appropriate, discussion of specific BMT-related problems will be included below.

Psycho-oncology aspects of medical oncology

Needle phobia

In many cases, chemotherapy must be given intravenously (injected into your veins). Usually, this is done slowly over minutes to hours. It will, inevitably, involve having a needle inserted in your arm. Some patients absolutely dread this. Some even consider refusing treatment as they are so frightened of needles. They are often referred to us in psycho-oncology as having 'needle phobias' – an extreme fear, sometimes panic, of having bloods taken or a needle inserted in their arm. Under normal circumstances, 'phobias' can be successfully treated with a graded psychological intervention (behaviour therapy). However, there is no time to deliver this in the context of chemotherapy for cancer. Patients need to start on their treatment as soon as possible.

In this context (the need to move on with your cancer treatment), please see the information points below:

- As in all the stories we have heard already, please make sure to talk to your team about your fears. They will understand. They will have encountered this many times before, and will be able to help you.
- In cases of overwhelming anxiety/panic, your cancer doctors can prescribe a very effective anti-anxiety drug for you. These are not without problems, so doctors generally prescribe sparingly, but sometimes 'needs must', and they are certainly very effective.

- As a doctor who has treated severe phobias of all kinds using psychological treatments, there are several helpful points to note about anxiety and panic:
  - Despite the feeling that it is catastrophic and overwhelming, extreme anxiety rarely lasts for more than 20 minutes and does not result in collapse. In fact, the anxiety triggers such an adrenaline surge that your blood pressure and pulse go up, not down, so you are very unlikely to faint (with one exception – see final point in this section).
  - With repeated attendance (exposure) to the feared situation (in this case needles), the anxiety reduces each time, as your body (and mind) habituate to the fact that you can do it.
  - Pointers to help you 'get through':
    - Ideally, lie down (with your feet up) while the needle is inserted/bloods are taken.
    - Look away (do not try to see the needle/blood being taken).
    - If feeling 'woozy', wait until you feel steady before standing up again.
  - All chemotherapy nurses are highly trained in giving chemotherapy and will be well used to managing this situation.
- The **'exception'**: there is one (rare) condition (blood-injury phobia) associated with a reduction in blood pressure (fainting) if the person sees blood. This is a very unusual condition and often runs in families. It can be successfully treated using a complex behaviour-therapy programme. But, again, in the constraints of

needing rapid chemotherapy, this is not an option. It can be successfully managed using the suggestions above (lying flat etc).

Finally, in over 20 years of working with patients with cancer, I have never seen a patient who gets the help above unable to receive their treatment because of 'needle phobia'.

Nausea, sickness, vomiting

Chemotherapy can be associated with nausea – a feeling of sickness and vomiting. Few people who have not experienced this can understand how wearing and debilitating constant nausea is. It takes over every aspect of one's thoughts and life. The minute one wakens until one goes to sleep, the constant feeling of 'seasickness' is there. While this can occur with most chemotherapy regimens, it is often worse for those in the BMT unit, on high-dose chemotherapy, isolated in a single room

What can be done to help? Like everything else, while it seems impossible at the time, it is important to say that this too will pass and you will eventually be able to eat, drink and enjoy food again. In the meantime, please let your medical team know as soon as possible if you are nauseated. There are now many excellent drugs to combat nausea. Immediate treatment with anti-nausea drugs (often now automatically given with or before chemotherapy) is important as psychological factors – fear and anxiety – can make nausea worse. Certainly, the two interact to magnify each other. That is why an understanding that it may happen and is a relatively 'normal' though deeply unpleasant side-effect is important. Furthermore, your team may decide to use **anti-anxiety drugs** as well as anti-nausea drugs to help. These issues are particularly important if you have ever had trouble eating in the past, such as an eating disorder. Please ensure you talk to your team as you are likely to need additional support to maintain your eating.

Gut effects – mouth ulcers, difficulty swallowing, diarrhoea

These side-effects are more common with high-dose chemotherapy, such as BMT. One of the possible side-effects of chemotherapy is that it can damage the cells lining your gut, causing soreness and ulcers on the inside of your mouth and further down your gut lining. This can make eating and drinking, even talking, sometimes even swallowing your own saliva, difficult. Particularly if you are admitted for BMT, if you are on regular medication before oncology treatment, please let your team know in advance as they may have to give them to you in some other way if you cannot swallow them. While it can be difficult, follow the routines for cleaning your mouth and gums every day. It can help to reduce the ulceration and soreness.

The ulceration can also cause diarrhoea, which is very wearing, exhausting and humiliating for patients, often so weak they find it difficult to get to the toilet. While it can seem impossible to believe at the time, it will get better and, while it may seem small compensation at the time, it is a sign that the drugs are doing their job. Tell your family that these things may happen. Plan with them whether you would like them to just come and sit with you, particularly if you are an in-patient – and warn them you may be too tired, weak and exhausted to chat and engage with them – but you will appreciate their presence. Make sure they know you may feel unable to even have them visit. They should know that this simply reflects how exhausted you may be and that you will still be depending on, and valuing, their support.

Hair loss (alopecia)

One possible side-effect of chemotherapy is hair loss. Thankfully, many of the cancer treatments now can be modified to reduce this risk and there have also been several advances in prevention (for example scalp cooling) that have reduced the number of people who develop alopecia.

Some people do not find hair loss distressing, others find it very distressing. As always, it is the meaning of the side-effect for them that must be understood if we are to help.

Aged 32, Helen was referred to the Psycho-oncology service for management of distress. Her team were unclear why she had become so distressed as her chemotherapy treatment was going well. However, it seemed to be related to the recent onset of hair loss.

Helen was initially overwhelmed during her psycho-oncology assessment. She was devastated by her cancer diagnosis. A quiet private person, she hated the intrusion of illness and treatments into her life. Even more so, she had dreaded losing her hair. She recognised that this did not seem to make sense. Why would she focus on hair loss when she could lose her life?

Further discussion about this over the next few sessions provided a link between her sense of privacy and the intrusive unwanted attention of others, particularly strangers. For her, the loss of her hair was about loss of herself, her identity, what she perceived as her femininity. Even worse, for her, was the implicit public announcement that she was A PERSON WITH CANCER. She hated the attention, the sideways looks, the misplaced sympathetic comments.

One of the things she examined during her sessions in psycho-oncology was why she found this public display of her vulnerability so difficult: why did she feel so angry about people's responses, what she perceived as their 'pity'? She identified a loss of control, feeling a victim.

Having identified and verbalised her underlying fears, she decided to take practical steps to 'turn around' her experience, to 'own it' as opposed to having it 'own her'. She started an extensive collection of exotic, beautiful, silk scarves to wrap around her head. When her hair started to grow back, she showed her shaven look as a new fashion statement.

The situation was not without its challenges. Occasionally, she still became overwhelmed. And, inevitably, an ill-judged remark from a stranger, or even a relative, would precipitate major distress. Overall, though, she described how, once she had examined what was driving her distress and taken control of the situation herself, she found she could better manage it.

Fatigue, weakness, exhaustion

With time, as some of the acute effects of chemotherapy wear off, you may find yourself feeling slightly better in some respects, less nausea, less diarrhoea, but you may feel exhausted, tired and weak. This will be particularly pronounced if you have been bed-bound for days at a time, with little or no use of your muscles. Inevitably, when you go to move, stand up or even sit up, you may find yourself dizzy and weak. People often become frightened by this, feeling it is yet another sign of the cancer taking over. These symptoms are an (almost) inevitable result of lying in bed for several weeks – your muscles, your usual physical reaction systems have been 'turned off' and you will have been considerably weakened by chemotherapy (and infections). So, while feelings of failure, demoralisation and despair are understandable, please be aware that the weakness, dizziness and fatigue are simply effects of what you have experienced over the previous few weeks. Your team will be well used to seeing this. Talk to your physiotherapist – they are excellent allies in helping you plan a (carefully graded) recovery. You will need a slow, steady, graded recovery.

Steroid 'psychosis'

We could not have a discussion on cancer treatments without specifically mentioning steroids. Steroids (such as prednisolone, dexamethasone) are drugs that are used in cancer for many reasons. They can be a key part of treatment for some blood cancers. They are also used to reduce side-effects of cancer treatment and to reduce and treat other symptoms, for example brain swelling. Like most drugs, therefore, they have some very beneficial effects (the reason they are prescribed). But they may also have some very significant unwanted effects, particularly on mental health

Aged 56, Oliver had a bone-marrow transplant for leukaemia. It had been a harrowing, difficult experience but it had ultimately gone well. He had survived. However, some weeks after his transplant, he needed high-dose steroids.

Initially, he thought they were 'great'. He suddenly had lots of energy, barely needed to sleep and developed great confidence in abilities that he had never had before. True, he did feel a bit more irritable than normal and his children and wife seemed more 'meddlesome' than usual – commenting on his driving (he felt he could safely drive faster than usual), and seeming very upset when he got up extra early one morning (3 o'clock) to rewire the electricity in the house. It seemed to him an easy task as his thinking had become so clear. Oliver's wife, however, was extremely concerned. With some difficulty, she got him to agree to attend his consultant for urgent review. His cancer consultant recognised the effect of steroids and referred him for an urgent psycho-oncology assessment that afternoon.

I saw Oliver and his wife that afternoon. His wife was distraught about Oliver's behaviour, feeling that he was taking extreme risks, and making plans that he would not normally make. She felt that any attempt by her to intervene led to Oliver becoming angry and dismissive – very unusual behaviour for him. She also noticed that he rarely slept, pacing the house at night-time, sending emails, making phone calls, doing things that she felt he would regret in the future.

Oliver, on the other hand, felt that everything was fine. In fact, he was slightly irked that he had been referred for assessment. He felt full of energy, had 'great ideas', showed me a book where he had written complex plans for the future. I could see he was having difficulty sitting still during the assessment. He was tense and became irritable on several occasions. He did agree that he was having extreme difficulty in sleeping, and that while he was 'on the go' constantly, he was feeling exhausted, yet could not rest. After some discussion about steroids and their effects, and, supported by his cancer doctor who did not want to stop his steroids, Oliver agreed to take some medication to combat these effects of his steroids. The effect was almost instantaneous. For the first time in weeks, Oliver was able to sleep, his sense of being constantly alert lessened, and he began to rest. He had agreed to allow his wife to also give feedback and she confirmed what he had said, noting that his impulsivity had also reduced.

Oliver's story and response to steroids is not unusual. Steroids initially give people a 'boost'. They feel they have more energy, often feel more 'positive'. However, very quickly, in some people, this can escalate and these 'positive' effects spin out of control. People describe feeling constantly restless, needing to be 'on the go' even though they are exhausted. Usually, they cannot sleep, or only sleep for 1 or 2 hours a night, lying awake with their thoughts racing. Occasionally, like Oliver, they begin to over-inflate their abilities – driving recklessly, taking excessive risks, spending impulsively, taking on projects they normally would never do. One lady, whose behaviour had, uncharacteristically, become loud, inappropriate and disinhibited, was absolutely distraught when her behaviour settled and she realised what had happened.

This is an **effect of steroids on mood** (unhelpfully, incorrectly, often called steroid psychosis). In effect, steroids induce a form of 'mania' – a well-described mood disorder that, for some people, arises spontaneously as a mental illness. For those on steroids, it only happens when they are on steroids, but the effects can be serious.

What to do about steroid-induced mania?

The first step is to be educated about it – to know it can happen, to be aware of the early signs, and **to ask for help early on.** Below are some points to note:

- Difficulty sleeping (insomnia) (severe) is one of the earliest warning signs. Anyone who starts on steroids and who notices a sudden worsening in their sleep should discuss it with their treating doctor.
- People with steroid-induced mania symptoms do not recognise it themselves. This is particularly problematic. Usually the person thinks they are 'fine'. That is why they take on tasks like rewiring the house with no prior experience. This means that it can be very difficult to get them to accept there is a problem and to take treatment. Things to help include:
  - Be sure to tell your family/supports about these effects, ask them to discuss it with your doctor so there is an agreement that they will act in your interest and on your behalf if necessary by alerting your team.
  - Get treatment early. Steroid-induced mania is eminently treatable, but the earlier the intervention, the more rapid the response, and the less likely that the situation will deteriorate.
- There is a successful treatment for steroid-induced mania. Sleeping tablets, valium and other drugs do not work. It requires treatment with a special group of drugs

(tablets) known as 'antipsychotics', which are normally used in mainstream psychiatry for mania. Patients who are treated with these drugs (at appropriate doses) for steroid-induced mania report an immediate feeling of calming, their sleep settled, their irritability gone. However, when they research the drug on the internet, they immediately fear they are 'psychotic' and will never get better. It is very important that you understand that this is a temporary drug-induced situation that will get better as soon as the drug (steroids) stop. Because the drugs to treat steroid-induced mania are not usually within the experience of most oncologists, they will often refer you to a psychiatrist for advice and help to manage it.

- The other possible intervention is to stop the steroids. However, as steroids are so often a necessary or very important part of the cancer treatment, this is rarely the best option. Careful co-management is usually best – discuss this with your cancer team.

Hormone treatments – hot flushes, premature menopause, infertility, anxiety, depression

Anyone taking hormone treatments for cancer will recognise this group of symptoms as often being associated with hormone treatments. Some of these symptoms have multiple causes that may, or may not, include the hormone treatment. Others, such as hot flushes, premature menopause or infertility may be more directly related. Side-effects depend on which hormone treatment you are getting. Please discuss with your cancer team – it is their role to reflect and consider whether the side-effect you are experiencing is related to a specific drug.

Others

There will inevitably be physical side-effects of oncology treatments not listed here. The most important message to give is to please discuss these with your cancer team – early and often. They will be best placed to understand the links between your symptoms and your treatment and how best to manage them. Often patients say they do not want to bother a busy team. It is ultimately better, for you and for them, to ask for the information.

6

Cancer Treatments – Surgery and Radiotherapy

Surgery

Surgery is an important treatment for cancer. Every operation is tailored for the cancer and the individual. Make sure to ask your surgeon to explain specifically what operation you will have. A diagram can be very helpful. As always, if you can have a relative with you, please do, as they are much more likely to remember the information.

For most people, surgery is a relatively uncomplicated procedure. However, like all treatments, it can have unwanted effects. Information will be key – both in knowing what may lie ahead, and in understanding how best to manage the impact of whatever may happen. Some of the more common fears and concerns reported by patients are discussed below. Some of these are minor; others have more major impacts.

Tubes and drains

It is likely that you will have a tube or drain left in place after surgery. These are usually there to help you to recover more quickly and efficiently. Rather than seeing them as frightening objects, you can regard them as helping you. Nonetheless, they can be very disconcerting, and sometimes painful. Ask your surgeon what drains might need to be put in, where they will be, and, roughly, how long they will be in. Make sure your family know about them as well, as it can be very disconcerting for your family to arrive to find you with several rather frightening-looking drains in place after surgery, particularly if they didn't expect it.

Intensive care (ICU)

There is no doubt that ICU can be a very frightening place. Large machines, loud noises, recurrent bleeps, alarms that seem to go off incessantly and, in ICUs with several beds in one area, the vision of what seems like alarmingly ill people around you. As one patient said to me, *'I opened my eyes, looked around and thought – am I really that bad? These people all look to be at death's door.'* Added to this is the feeling of disorientation as you regain consciousness after surgery, only gradually becoming aware (and remembering) what has happened. Ideally, find out everything you can in advance. Might you need to go to ICU? Is it possible to visit the ICU area before surgery?

Complex ICU care

For most patients, after elective (planned) surgery, their stay in ICU is brief and uncomplicated. For a few, particularly after emergency surgery, it may be more difficult.

Rasa was referred to the Psycho-oncology service by a senior cancer clinician who had been looking after her for several months. When I initially saw her for assessment, she was so agitated she could not sit on a chair in my office. Instead, I had to take her history as we walked up and down the corridors of the building. She found it extremely difficult to tell her story. With poor English, ashamed and humiliated by her experience, she was initially not willing to trust me with any details. She did agree that she was extremely distressed, and to allow me to have an interpreter attend the next session, when she told her story in more detail.

Aged 28, single, she had only recently moved to Ireland, her English was still quite poor and she had very few friends or supports locally. Shortly after moving, she discovered that she had cancer and needed very complex surgery. After surgery, she became very unwell and was moved urgently to Intensive Care (ICU). With a very high fever, unable to catch her breath, shivering uncontrollably, she felt very confused. 'Where was she? Who were these people trying to hold her down and stick something down her throat? Were they trying to harm her?' She fought against them with all her strength. Some days later, awake in ICU with a tube in her throat, she still felt confused and disorientated. She struggled to breathe as they tried to take the tube away. Terrified, she could not fully understand what people were saying.

Rasa's condition had improved over the next few days. Her confusion cleared. She was transferred to a regular ward and discharged home. She remained physically well and her cancer reviews were positive with the cancer 'cured'.

However, what Rasa could not discuss was the terror of her nights at home – the fear that enveloped her as soon as she closed her eyes, the images of herself 'drowning', unable to breathe, striking out at hands trying to grab her. Her sense of shame at her behaviour, her fear that she had 'gone mad', coupled with her difficulty in expressing herself, meant that she could not, would not, discuss it at her out-patient reviews.

Things got worse. She was too afraid to go to bed at night, spending her nights sitting in a chair. She now had periods in the day as well as the night when the images would come back, often triggered by a noise, a smell, a memory. She began to find it difficult to stay indoors, to sit in a room. She couldn't eat. Going to the hospital for reviews brought it all back. She was convinced she was going 'mad', distressed and humiliated by her experiences. Finally, Rasa managed to tell her cancer consultant. She was referred to us at Psycho-oncology for help.

Rasa's story was a story of post-traumatic stress disorder (PTSD) (a complex psychological reaction to extreme stress) following a period of confusion (delirium).

Hearing an explanation, and names, for her symptoms significantly reduced Rasa's fears. She responded well to treatment, although needed several months of out-patient treatment, combining medication and psychological intervention. Ultimately, her medication was discontinued and she was discharged from the service.

Admission to ICU is a frightening experience for many people, particularly if it is an emergency transfer when they have become suddenly unwell. This is made worse if, like Rasa, people become **confused** (sometimes called '**delirium**'). People lose track of days and time, they can become unsure about where they are, overwhelmed with a sense of panic, fear and distrust. Understanding that all of this happens in the context of confusion – a not uncommon response to infection and/or medication – is the first step to recovery. Confusion is usually short-lived and goes away completely when the underlying problem is treated.

After the operation – exhaustion and demoralisation

'Waking up' after surgery, finding it has gone well, that your cancer has been removed, is clearly good news. However, for some, the post-operative period is tempered by feelings of exhaustion and demoralisation that hamper recovery. This can be worsened by a (completely unwarranted) sense of shame and guilt at not being more 'grateful' for the good news.

Aged 66, Tim had always prized himself on being 'a coper'. A highly educated man, an academic and a teacher, he had always been full of energy and 'met everything head-on'. He had not expected a diagnosis of oesophageal cancer at the age of 66, three months after his retirement. He was determined to 'beat it' and attacked his treatment plan with his usual rigour and enthusiasm. He needed complex surgery that lasted several hours, but he 'knew he could manage it', and looked forward to returning to sport and his friends in the weeks afterwards.

Three weeks after his operation, Tim could barely get from his bed to a chair. He felt exhausted, weak and, most difficult for him, utterly helpless. Loss of his independence made him demoralised and despondent. He could not face eating, feeling increasingly nauseated over time. Over the next three weeks he found it diffi-cult to motivate himself to eat, get dressed, get out of bed. He knew he was losing weight and condition. This made him even more demoralised. Now he felt that cancer (ironically now 'gone', removed by surgery) had destroyed him, changed him forever – his pride in his abilities, his sense of self – gone.

One of the first, most important things for Tim was understanding that, as is often the case, what he was experiencing was very common. He had had very major surgery and needed time to recover. His operation was like 'being hit a bus – that then reversed over him and hit him again' (although he did not repeat this analogy to his surgeon). He needed to acknowledge this and build a realistic programme for recovery, with supervision and support from his psycho-oncology team, his nutritionist and a detailed rehabilitation programme with his physiotherapist.

Within a matter of weeks, he had made enough improvement to arrive at his out-patient reviews seeking ways to help others by sharing his experience.

Tim's story – his irritation, self-loathing, impatience, feeling he had 'lost himself' – can happen when people do not fully realise the impact that surgery will have. It is, of course, a delicate balance. Post-operative care is focused, rightly, on rapid rehabilitation to minimise risks but, as always, the individual patient's 'persona' will need to be factored into any plan. Some will need to be gently supported in moving on; others, like Tim, will need to be gently brought back to a more realistic level.

Surgery and specific cancer sites

Some of the effects of surgery relate to the operation 'site'. Head and neck surgery, for example, may be associated with significant changes in appearance and/or difficulties in speaking, eating and drinking. Bowel surgery may mean you have a 'bowel bag' – something that you will need help and information to understand and manage (your cancer team will help you with this information).

Radiotherapy

Radiation therapy (radiotherapy) uses specific, tailored radiation to kill cancer cells. It is a common form of treatment for some cancers, often used together with surgery and/or chemotherapy, sometimes used on its own. Radiotherapy is usually given in short bursts, once daily, over several days. The length of treatment (a treatment 'course') depends on the type of cancer and the aims of the treatment, but is usually weeks, often six to twelve weeks. Each treatment session is quite short, lasting minutes (around 5 minutes), although the overall session may last up to thirty minutes while the therapist places you in the correct position and sets up the machine. You will need to lie still during treatment. You can usually get your treatment as an out-patient. You will not be 'radioactive' or pose a risk to others after treatment.

Radiotherapy planning sessions

Generally, when having radiotherapy, you will first have a 'treatment planning session' before your treatment starts. You will need to lie in a machine like a scanning machine, allowing the team to 'see' your cancer and plan exactly where to deliver the radiation. The radiation therapist will then mark the area for treatment using a 'tattoo', or ink marks. If you are getting radiation treatment to your face or head, you may need to be fitted for a mask. The mask contains lots of air holes as you will need to wear it each time you have treatment to ensure your head is in the exact same position each time. During each treatment session, the machine will make a noise and move around. You will be on your own in the room, but the therapist will be just outside, guiding the machine, watching through a window, and able to speak to you through a microphone (very similar to when you were having scans and X-rays).

The more common psychological difficulties described by patients getting radiotherapy include claustrophobia, fatigue and body-image problems, discussed below.

Claustrophobia

Claustrophobia, fear of enclosed spaces, like 'needle phobia', is a somewhat unhelpful term, as it conjures up images of a dreadful condition over which patients have no control. Fear (some patients would say 'terror') of enclosed spaces is, nonetheless, a major issue for some patients.

As with needle phobia, claustrophobia is normally treated with a structured psychological intervention. However, again like needle phobia, in the context of cancer, there just is not enough time to correctly use this treatment. A combination of methods: support by the nursing and radiation team, full explanation and visits beforehand, and appropriate medication means that patients, despite their worst fears, can go ahead to get radiation treatment successfully.

Radiation-induced fatigue

Fatigue is generally a late effect of cancer treatment, and is discussed more fully in a later chapter. It is, however, a relatively common short-term effect with radiotherapy. Because the effects of radiation are, generally, not visible, patients are often surprised by how tiring the treatment is. This is especially so over time – the effect accumulates over weeks. It generally reduces over time, with short periods of rest.

Radiation tattoos

Radiation 'tattoos' – skin ink markings to mark the places where the treatment is directed – are one way in which radiation treatment leaves 'visible' marks that can cause distress. While considered insignificant by some, others find the visible tattoos signs that 'mark them out', making them feel 'like a victim', 'vulnerable' to others, distressing. As with so many examples, often it is the thoughts behind the fears that are the real driver of the worry. One patient described having felt completely overwhelmed with these tattoos – not wanting to leave her house, avoiding family and friends. One day she met another lady waiting for radiotherapy, with the same tattoos. The lady noticed her looking at them and said, *'I know – they mark me out. I have cancer. But they are also the marks that are directing the treatment to destroy it. And that gives me strength.'* That simple conversation was enough to help her change her thought patterns and manage her distress about the tattoos.

Brief treatment times

One of the 'positive' aspects of radiotherapy is the (usually) short time it lasts – brief weeks. Ironically, this can also be one of its disadvantages. With medical treatment, attendance at the day ward over several months, while long, allows people to develop strong informal support networks, to build a sense of community with others who understand their situation. They also have time to develop close links with their treating teams. While patients getting radiation usually have excellent relationships with their teams, because their time attending is short they do not have the same chances to develop support over prolonged periods. For most patients, this is a disadvantage they are happy to accept as they want to spend as little time as possible in treatment.

Section III

THE IMPACT OF CANCER

7

Cancer and Thoughts – the Cancer Myths

Our thoughts are intensely powerful. They control how we feel, how we behave. Yet our thoughts are not always correct. Thoughts are not facts. Thoughts are simply the way we see, perceive or understand things, at that particular moment. They are affected by our previous experiences, the information (or misinformation) we have, our hopes, our feelings. It is not the situation in which we find ourselves that makes us think, feel or behave in a certain way, it is how we understand, or make sense of, the situation. Often this is due to the myths we have inherited.

Just because we think something is true, that does not mean it is true

Many of you will have read that sentence and said, 'well yes, obviously'. But the reality is much of the time we automatically 'jump to conclusions', don't even think about it, just assume something is true when it may not be. We don't usually spend time thinking of all the possible alternative explanations. We see, we react, we move on. Much of the time, that is okay, we get by. But, when we are anxious or low, these reactions can become distorted, contaminating our feelings and our reactions.

When you have cancer, your stress and distress puts severe pressure on your ability to filter and interpret information. Even worse, quite often you may have inherited several cancer myths so that the information you start with is biased.

This chapter presents some of the cancer myths, followed by some of the filters, and interpretations that patients have told us about. These can hugely add to the burden of cancer. In reading about them, you can reflect – are they part of your (mis)information systems? Are there alternatives? Information is only powerful if it is the correct information, appropriate for you. Misinformation can be very destructive.

Cancer myths – the tyranny of misinformation

I am always wary when I hear someone start a sentence with 'apparently with cancer you should...' There are so many **unhelpful myths about cancer** – unhelpful either because they are often simply untrue or unproven and/or they are statements that are entirely unhelpful for someone struggling to manage in the face of a cancer diagnosis.

The **list of myths below** includes those I have heard most commonly. There are undoubtedly many more. A general rule when considering these is to ask yourself, 'Is this actually true? Is this helpful? How much can I change?'

There are, of course, some statements that are true, helpful, even essential for some cancers – stopping smoking in the context of lung cancer is one, avoiding the sun with skin cancer is another. So perhaps the first thing, if you are uncertain, is to ask your cancer doctor if there is any evidence for the statement, and then assess how helpful it will be for you to follow that lead.

I must be 'positive' all the time if I am going to beat cancer

Some people think that there is a 'correct' way to cope with cancer – the more positive and optimistic they are the more likely they will be cured. Worse, they may believe that being angry or sad, having any 'negative' emotions may cause their cancer to 'grow more', or to 'come back'. These beliefs are not only false, they are extremely unhelpful. It is inevitable that people will feel sad, angry or depressed at times, particularly in the context of cancer. Adding the belief that by feeling this way they are responsible for their cancer coming back is hugely damaging. Like many other scenarios in this book, there is no one 'correct' way to manage cancer. Generally, the way people manage reflects their own unique personal style of coping over many years, prior to ever getting a cancer diagnosis. It has, usually, served to get you this far in life and you are unlikely to change hugely at this point. Yes, it is not helpful if you have collapsed in distress, unable to function, to get your treatment. But it is unrealistic to expect you must be positive all the time.

My personality, coping style or stress caused my cancer

Some people believe that certain personalities, coping styles, childhood experiences or stress cause all cancers. This has **not** been persuasively supported by research studies. Furthermore, it is an extremely unhelpful belief for our patients.

When something bad happens, we all tend to search for a reason, an explanation. Finding something to blame gives a sense of security – we can prevent this happening again. But it can also increase a sense of guilt, sadness, anger, regret – very unhelpful emotions for someone with cancer. It may be, that in the future, people decide to review their lives in the context of having had cancer – many people find this very helpful, a form of regrowth after trauma – but that is a different concept.

Cancer kills everyone who gets it

Thankfully, few people believe this now. Almost everyone recognises that many, many people with cancer recover, and recover fully. Survival rates and treatments are improving all the time. It is also very important to remember that there are many, many different types of cancer. Even in the 'same' area – for example lung cancer – there are different types. So, never, ever compare yourself to someone else.

Talking to my partner or family about my feelings will only upset them

People with cancer often want to protect their family or friends by 'putting on a brave face' or even not really telling them at all what is happening. Please know now that **they almost certainly already know**. They will certainly know, if they are close to you, that something is seriously wrong. I cannot tell you the number of times I have seen a patient to have them say to me, 'Now, do not tell X how bad things are, I don't want to upset them,' only for me to meet X, who then says to me, 'Now, I think she does not really know how bad things are, so I don't want to discuss it with her.'

Hiding information, and your distress, from people you care about is hugely stressful and very difficult. It is also, almost certainly, a waste of time. If they are close to you, they already know. Furthermore, you are denying yourself a huge amount of necessary support – support that will help you to get through and get better. And you are denying them the chance of helping you, and speaking frankly to you.

My memory has been damaged (forever) because of 'chemo-brain'

Careless, 'trip-off-the-tongue', pseudo-scientific terms are potentially enormously damaging. Precisely because of their pseudo-scientific nature, many patients take these terms as absolute fact. The abilities to focus, pay attention and concentrate are enormously impaired if you are tired, exhausted and feeling unwell. Ask anyone who has had a bad experience with flu. And if you cannot pay attention and concentrate, you cannot register information, so you definitely cannot recall it. Difficulties with registration and recall are also all worsened by anxiety. So we now have the 'perfect storm' for causing both distress and difficulties for patients. Yes, your attention, registration, concentration and, as a result, your memory may be worse than usual at present. This is entirely to be expected and will improve as you become physically stronger and any other underlying physical or psychological problems are treated.

Of course, there will always be some situations where

memory or other skills may be affected directly by cancer or its treatment, but these are generally very specific examples, and do not apply to the vast number of patients with cancer.

My energy levels have been damaged forever because of cancer

Cancer-related fatigue is extremely common both during and after treatment. There are numerous causes – physical and psychological, cancer- and/or cancer-treatment-related. Many people believe that fatigue is an 'inevitable price' they have paid for surviving their cancer. This is not the case. To adapt to their new state, many patients sleep frequently during the day and stop almost all activities during treatment and may continue this after treatment has ended. This can cause another 'perfect storm', as ceasing activity and poor sleep patterns can worsen fatigue. Energy levels can be improved with help and guidance from your cancer team and/or psycho-oncology team (discussed in a later chapter).

An absence of social support will reduce my lifespan

There is no doubt that having a good social network is, generally, very helpful in the context of cancer, in fact in most contexts. This is both for the practical support that families and friends can bring, and for the positive effects of social interaction. But all kinds of people get cancer. And that includes people who have always preferred their own company, pursuing a relatively solitary existence. That is fine. If that describes you, you are not suddenly going to change into an extrovert, constantly seeking company. As always, it is a question of looking at what works for you, what you will find useful, and getting the help you need. This may include practical support from others, or from your cancer team.

Cancer and mental health myths

Sadly, there also remain many myths about mental health and mental ill-health that stigmatise and intensify the suffering of people who experience mental illness. For those with cancer and psychological distress, these myths are intensified.

Mary sat in my office, blinking back the tears. In a low quiet voice that she struggled to keep steady, she told her story.

All her life, she had feared becoming mentally ill. Her father had had a diagnosis of 'manic-depression' and had spent much of his life in 'mental institutions'. She had always dreaded that she would need to see a psychiatrist. For her, the stigma and shame would be unbearable.

Her other fear was that she would get cancer. Her mother had died of breast cancer. Somehow, Mary had equated that with a further failure and a sense of shame. She stopped and looked me in the eye. 'So here I am,' she said quietly, 'talking to a psychiatrist about my diagnosis of breast cancer – a double whammy. I did not even tell my husband I was coming to see you. I got him to drop me at the Cancer Day Ward for "tests".'

It is hard to see suffering and stigma driven by myths and misinformation. Cancer is a difficult enough diagnosis on its own, without the myths. Anyone whom I have looked after who has experienced both severe mental illness (for example steroid-induced mania or severe depression) and cancer has said to me, *'I would prefer to have my cancer back than ever to have to go through that again.'*

But the myths and false beliefs about psychological distress and cancer continue.

Only 'weak' people seek psychological care

It is a source of huge distress for any mental-health worker to see the ongoing stigma that exists about asking for help, particularly help for mental health. It is, of course, an example of such contradictory beliefs that people are willing to (appropriately) take large amounts of 'cancer treatments' that can damage their gut, their hair, their general health, but absolutely will not countenance getting support for their mental well-being. No one is exempt from needing help. For everyone there is a 'tipping point'.

Jeremy was struggling with his cancer treatment – prolonged, difficult and complex – and he was now utterly exhausted. He was referred to psycho-oncology by his cancer doctor, a senior physician with a very good understanding of the complex inter-actions between mental and physical health. She noted that, even though Jeremy was doing well from a cancer perspective, he was finding his rehabilitation very difficult.

Jeremy, a retired naval officer, was very unhappy at discussing his problems with a psycho-oncologist. Abrupt in manner, utterly forthright, he made clear that he really did not want to speak to a psychiatrist, perceiving this as a sign of 'weakness'. He 'shouldn't need' psychological help. He had reluctantly agreed 'out of respect for' his cancer doctor. His psycho-oncologist knew that, without Jeremy's engagement in the process, nothing would help. After some thought, she asked Jeremy to forgive her for using a (grossly) simplified military example. 'If you were in battle, hugely outnumbered, with access to troops nearby for which you could send and ask for help,' she asked, 'what would you do? Would you fight on knowing you would lose? Or would you send for help?'

Initially irritated by this simplistic example, he snapped, 'Of course one would ask for help. One would be a fool not to use all the resources available.'

Then he paused briefly, the first traces of a smile appearing as his own words sank in. 'Okay,' he said. 'I am listening.'

Jeremy ultimately needed very little intervention from the psycho-oncology service. He mainly benefited from support and guidance about the implementation of a realistic rehabilitation package of the type described in the chapter on cancer-related fatigue.

Without these simple interventions, however, he risked continuing in an ever-increasing downward spiral of depression, demoralisation and despair, fuelling his increasing inactivity and withdrawal.

It is, of course, not only in cancer that the stigma about mental health is apparent. It is in the general community as well. Occasionally, we see patients who have struggled, alone and unaided, with mental illness in the community and only had it recognised and treated when it was noted by a sharp-eyed 'cancer doctor' who detected an underlying mental illness in addition to the patient's cancer.

Noel was a quiet, softly spoken man in his 50s. He had recently been diagnosed with cancer. His cancer doctor had referred him to psycho-oncology as he felt he had a significant mental illness, in addition to his cancer.

Noel described how, all his life, he had struggled with his 'head being full of worries'. He worried about everything – not getting his work done exactly right, not checking the locks an exact number of times, not checking the lights were off. He could not describe it, but if he did not check, or redo things, a set number of times, he had a huge sense of anxiety that something terrible would happen – and it would be his fault. Because of these fears and behaviours, he had dropped out of university, been unable to keep any 'job' going and, in recent years, mainly stayed at home. He had realised he probably needed help for this but the stigma of seeking help for mental illness was more than he could bear. When diagnosed with cancer by his GP, he had readily agreed to see the cancer doctor and did not argue when he asked him to see the psychiatrist attached to the cancer team.

Noel had obsessive-compulsive disorder – an illness that had pervaded all aspects of his life for the previous 40 years. The psycho-oncology service provided a combination of psychological treatment and medication. Noel responded well and described how he felt well for the first time in his life. Despite his cancer diagnosis, he went back to university to study the subjects he had loved, and made his way through his degree course.

Noel's story is, in many ways, a shocking story. It required a diagnosis of cancer for his mental illness to be recognised. Stigma remains a major issue for people needing psychological support. One of the strengths of having psychological services integrated within medical ones, as with psycho-oncology, is that it helps to break down these barriers.

Cancer and treatment myths

There are also many myths about cancer treatment.

I should be grateful I have finished treatment
Many patients do NOT feel grateful when they finish treatment. For the first time, they have the space to stop and reflect on what has happened to them and they feel angry and upset. *'Why me? Why cancer? Why I am exhausted? I am never going to be the same again.'* Then they often feel guilty about not being grateful, which makes them feel worse.

Patients should not feel the need to be 'grateful' for finishing treatment. It is entirely understandable that they feel upset, angry, bereft, robbed – some of the many feelings that people describe. Of course, if they were able to step away from those (overwhelming) feelings, many would say they are glad their treatment is over, and thankful to those people (family, friends and cancer teams) who helped them to get there. But most are just too overwhelmed by all the other emotions.

I am not myself – I will never go back to being the way I was
Many patients pin their hopes on getting to the end of treatment and 'going back to the way they were'. While this is very understandable, it is not a very helpful plan. None of

us ever go backwards in time. Rarely do people consider going 'back' to themselves in time – except in the case of cancer or other major events in their lives. We can never go 'backwards'. Equally, however, it is not true to say that cancer has made someone into something or someone they are not. They are still the same person – albeit a person who has had a very traumatic diagnosis and difficult treatment; a person for whom life has certainly changed and, with it, many of the old certainties. This is not the same as saying they are 'a different person'.

I am a failure for not 'bouncing back'

Along with all the trauma of cancer and its treatment, patients add to their distress by blaming themselves for many things, one of which is that they 'should be better' than they are. This is why it is so important to know that **ending treatment is just the start of rehabilitation**. You have not 'bounced back' after treatment, because you are 'flattened', 'on the ground', exhausted and demoralised. You need time, help and support to recover. You have survived the 'active treatment' phase – now you need support, kindness and help to rehabilitate yourself back to functioning again.

Everyone else is managing so much better than me

As a clinician, there were certain 'cancer recovery' books that I would have liked to ban. I would listen to my patients recounting stories of 'inspirational' people they had read about – climbing mountains, wrestling bears to the ground single-handed (or whatever the equivalent is) two days after extensive cancer surgery, while my patient, unsurprisingly, was finding it difficult to just get out of a chair. I accept I may be exaggerating – but not by much! I am certain that this inspirational person is not actually doing what is described. Or, if they are, they are a very unusual person with unique supports. Yes, I accept everyone needs inspiration, but regular achievable inspiration would be helpful.

The reality is that everyone recovers at a different pace – there is neither a 'medal' nor 'shame' waiting at the end of the path. Furthermore, if everyone I am seeing thinks everyone else is doing better (often the case), then someone, somewhere is wrong. I see many people who struggle hugely. That is a fact of much of cancer treatment. Every cancer, every treatment is different. There is absolutely no point in comparing yourself with everyone else. You will either find someone who is doing better, which may lead you to feel humiliated and demoralised, or find someone who is doing worse, which will make you worry that you too will fall into the difficulties that they have. And the reality is you never ever know what is going on behind closed doors. So focus on yourself, your progress, your strategies. That is energy-consuming enough.

Cancer and thinking 'errors'

So far in this chapter we have been discussing unhelpful beliefs in cancer – myths and misinformation associated with cancer. There are also thinking 'errors' or **patterns of thinking** that can be unhelpful. These are not specific to cancer. This concept of thinking 'errors' was first extensively described by a psychiatrist called Aaron **Beck** and was used to develop a specific type of psychological treatment – cognitive behaviour therapy (CBT). These particular styles of thinking influence our behaviour. At its simplest, some of us are eternal optimists, others eternal pessimists – some see danger at every point, others sail happily through life, never even considering dangers. Often we have found our thinking styles helpful, they have suited our personality. Those of us who are cautious, for example, prefer to see danger in advance, modifying our lives to accommodate this. Our thinking patterns are, there-fore, often deeply ingrained. When we are distressed or stressed, as, for example, with cancer, our thinking patterns can become magnified and distorted. In these situations, we can make judgements that are not true, or, at least, not completely true. We can see problems where there may be none, can blow 'real' problems out of proportion, overestimate danger and setbacks, and underestimate our ability to cope. These thinking errors can make us feel low, anxious and angry. They can also cause us to behave in ways that may make things even more difficult for us.

Below are a few examples of the more common 'categories' of thinking errors that people may make, placed in the context of cancer. Often it is helpful to stop and consider if what you are thinking is a thinking 'error' and try to identify to which category it belongs. Doing this can help you to question the **truth** or, more importantly, the **helpfulness** of the thought. You will see that there are overlaps between the various styles.

All-or-nothing thinking (black and white thinking)
When we are distressed, we often view things as though there are only two possibilities – the world is seen in absolute 'black

and white', 'either/or' terms. For example, when hearing about the results of your treatment, if the answer is not '100% effective', one views it as 'useless'; or if one is not to the level one was at before cancer, one will never get to 'normal' – 'there is just no point'.

Imelda had been a very good hockey player before her cancer. She had worked hard at her hockey skills all her life, and maintained a very good level. Since finishing her cancer treatment, however, she was exhausted. She had made several efforts to return to hockey. In fact, plans to return to hockey were what had kept her 'sane' during her treatment. But now she could barely get out of the car, let alone play a match. She sat in her car, in the car park of the club, watching her team-mates, remembering what she used to be able to do, and fought back tears, sad and distressed. She would not, could not go through the humiliation of joining her team-mates. It was no good. She would never be back to where she was. And if she could not get back there, she would not play at all.

Imelda was distressed and angry about her situation. Getting back to hockey was what had kept her sane during her treatment and now she could not do it. Talking it through with her psycho-oncology team, identifying her thought processes, she created a rehabilitation programme for herself, acknowledging that this was a reasonable sporting approach. She also realised how humiliated she felt at having to start at the beginning again, and how this feeling was holding her back in her progress. Ultimately, after months of a rehabilitation programme, Imelda was back to playing hockey at her previous level – and better. She found she was now willing to take risks in her playing that she had not done before.

Overgeneralisation

No matter how much information you are given, you focus on the one negative event and decide that your case is a never-ending pattern of defeat and failure.

David had completely forgotten about his CT-scan appointment – until he got the letter from the hospital informing him that he had missed it. Previously he would have felt terrible, but would have said to himself, 'I was just too busy. That was foolish. I should have put it in my phone. I will phone to apologise and hopefully they will give me another appointment.' Now, having had cancer treatment, he said, 'This must be that "chemo-brain" I heard about. This is terrible. I will never recover from that. This is brain damage. I can never go back to work now. Everyone will realise my memory has gone and I cannot be relied on.'

Jumping to conclusions (thinking the worst)

When we are distressed, we tend to jump too quickly to negative conclusions. We believe certain bad things are about to happen without having any real facts and without considering other, more likely, options.

Ina had been sitting waiting to see her consultant in the outpatients. She knew she was not due for another hour but, always a 'worrier', she liked to be early to 'gather' herself. Suddenly she saw the nurse coming towards her. 'The doctor is going to see you early,' she said. 'They will call you in five minutes.' Ina's mind went into overdrive. 'It must be terrible news – they would never see me early otherwise. I have never been seen early before. My cancer is back – I knew it.'

Ina was in such a state by the time she got in that she could not hear a single word that was said. She heard the words 'remission', 'clear'; could see the doctor looking at her sympathetically (which confirmed her worst fears) but really could not make sense of what was being said.

Outside, Ina sat in the corridor, sobbing. It was only when a nurse came along and found her, that the situation was explained. There had been a cancellation and, because Ina was there early, she had been called in.

Ina's story is a very good example of jumping to (the worst) conclusions when distressed – and how this influenced her even after her visit had ended. Having someone with you at your appointment will help with this. If alone, taking time to write down what the doctor has said or asking a nurse to go over it with you afterwards may help.

Please be aware that much of what we are discussing in this last section forms the basic building blocks of a very specific, psychological treatment – cognitive behaviour therapy (CBT). For some of you, reading and understanding the process may be enough. Others may need to attend your psycho-oncology team for help. If unsure, please discuss with your team.

There is nothing I can do about my situation
This is, perhaps, the most unhelpful belief of all. It is, without doubt, very difficult to manage cancer and, particularly, to

manage the recovery from cancer. It can seem daunting, overwhelming, impossible, but there is always something that can be done. Enlist the help of your family, friends. Break it down into achievable steps. Identify goals. Make a plan. Note your progress. Remember to reward yourself for achievements along the way. If you are still struggling, you may need more expert help. Please speak to your cancer team. They are there to help.

8

Cancer and the Spectrum of Distress

Cancer-related distress – a 'normal reaction to an abnormal situation'

Almost everyone is 'distressed' in the face of a cancer diagnosis. The term '**distress**' is deliberately chosen. A broad term, it is easily understood by most people and includes the many different reactions to a cancer diagnosis. This distress, how people respond, varies hugely, and reflects their own individual coping style. Some are shocked and silent, others are tearful and overwhelmed, some are angry, many are afraid. Some, a small number seem to 'sail through' with little or no distress.

One of the key first steps in managing cancer-related distress is to understand what type of distress you have, as this should guide the intervention most likely to help you.

The cancer distress pyramid – a service model

Cancer-related distress can be thought of as existing on a spectrum, ranging from transient, mild distress that rapidly fades, to severe, persistent, pervasive distress, where one might encounter severe conditions that will need specific treatment, such as depression, anxiety or post-traumatic stress disorder (PTSD). As the response to cancer exists on a spectrum, so too the help or intervention must be available on a spectrum – the intervention should match the need.

When developing the psycho-oncology service for St James's Hospital, Dublin (SJH) with my colleague, Dr Sonya Collier, Clinical Psychologist, we initially struggled with how to set up a model for the service. We ultimately developed the service model shown in Figure 1. An inverted pyramid, it shows the varying levels and nature of possible cancer-related distress, with matched interventions. Transient mild distress (Level 1) is likely to be best helped by the support of family and friends, with education and support from the cancer teams. On the opposite end of the spectrum (the lowest level of the inverted pyramid, Level 5), severe conditions such as post-traumatic stress disorder, or steroid psychosis need rapid appropriate intervention that may combine the significant expertise of both clinical psychology and psychiatry, both medication and psychological treatments.

'Medicalising' 'normal' distress, a distress that is often adaptive and appropriate, is not only a misuse of resources, it may hamper people's ability to adapt. The model reminds us that the vast number of people with cancer are at the 'top of the pyramid', with transient distress (Level 1). Only a very small number, at the bottom of the pyramid, experience more severe responses. The clinicians at the bottom of the pyramid, with the most expertise in mental health (psycho-oncology) can support and educate cancer teams above them, who, in turn, support their patients. This model has since been incorporated into the most recent National Cancer Strategy for Ireland (Figure 1).

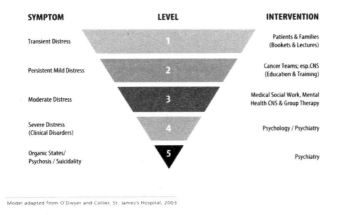

Model adapted from O'Dwyer and Collier, St. James's Hospital, 2003

Figure 1 The spectrum of distress and interventions – the St James's Hospital Psycho-oncology model

Why does this information matter for you?

I appreciate this may seem like far too much detail for someone with cancer, struggling to even read. However, sometimes patients, or families, are insistent that their relatives 'must see a psychiatrist' with distress, feeling that the support or education provided by their cancer teams are of 'no value'. If you are being treated by a well-supported cancer team, often this is not only enough, it is the right approach. So many times, information, education and support have been what patients have needed – and found sufficient – in managing their distress. If you are unclear, discuss with your cancer team.

95

The key first step, therefore, is to work out where you may lie on the cancer pyramid and then seek a treatment to match that.

How does cancer cause anxiety and depression?

It is a very difficult balance for people who have cancer. Most people with cancer have managed perfectly well before cancer struck. The experience of cancer and its treatment, however, can unsettle our usual coping mechanisms, transforming 'helpful' worry to long-lasting, pathological, unhelpful anxiety. Cancer can do this in different ways. For example, the experience of getting cancer can challenge someone's beliefs that if they look after themselves and are healthy in their habits, their health will be okay and they will not get cancer. With a cancer diagnosis, that sense of control and predictability vanishes. Or cancer may take away your normal coping strategies, for example exercise. If your 'rules for living' have suddenly been overturned, it is important to recognise that it is going to take you time to re-adjust. You may have to remodel a lifetime of daily 'thinking habits' that have generally served you well until now. For some people, time, reflection and support from family and friends are enough to help them adjust. Or you may 'remodel' your previous coping strategies. For now, a 5 km run with your friends becomes, instead, a social meeting twice a week. Over time, you will be able to reconstruct this, as you move out of the cancer treatment phase. But for now, you will need to adapt to your circumstances. It can be very difficult to do this alone – so please discuss with your team if you find you are struggling.

How to decide if help is needed

This is another difficult task. Mental health suffers from 'casual', 'inappropriate', incorrect use of words in everyday speech. "Depression', 'anxiety', even 'psychotic' are words that have slipped into everyday language so that it can be difficult to know when someone needs professional help. Depression is a core example of this. Someone who is 'depressed' may be a student who is 'fed up' because they have an exam in two days, the weather is fabulous and they would prefer to be outside enjoying the sunshine rather than stuck inside studying. Or it may mean someone who is struggling to come to terms with overwhelming grief from the death of a partner, or someone with a severe clinical depression needing specific psychiatric care and treatment.

As a general rule, as health professionals, we are concerned with the quality, severity and persistence of a particular mental state, as well as checking for specific features that may cause concern because they may suggest a more significant mental health problem.

Factors that suggest you are likely to need help, that the distress has become a more severe pathological problem, at the 'bottom of the pyramid', or the 'extreme' of the cancer-distress spectrum (and factors that every clinician considers) include:

- **Time** – if 'distress' has persisted for weeks or more.
- **Severity** – if distress is so severe that you cannot function, are unable to do the 'ordinary' things in life.

- **Particular features** – there are some features that are unusual or worrying for mental health practitioners – prominent feelings of **hopelessness**, **guilt**, **complete lack of enjoyment** of anything may suggest an evolving depression.
- **Unusual features** – very rarely, a small number of people have very 'strange' experiences – hearing voices or developing strange beliefs
- **Uncontrolled persistent use of substances** – such as alcohol or drugs – in a (misguided) effort to manage.

There are no 'hard and fast' rules about this. If you are concerned, please speak to your family or your cancer team. This is particularly important with mental health issues, because sometimes you yourself may be too distressed to recognise how things actually are. If your team are concerned, they can organise for a member of the psycho-oncology team to meet you.

Cancer and worry

Sometimes, with cancer, distress becomes anxiety rather than depression. Worry is, of course, a normal reaction to a difficult event. Everyone worries from time to time. **Worry** usually means being **concerned about an actual event or problem**, a **specific situation**, for example financial problems. **Worry can be helpful**, motivating us to act. We may 'worry' briefly, for example, as we see one of our close friends (or children) head off on a long international trip, knowing they will be gone, and possibly out of contact, for weeks. Generally, though, we can stop and contain that worry quickly, reasoning that there is little in our power to change what will happen.

Typically, when we use the term **anxiety** we are more focused on **'possible' events** or our beliefs about **things that might happen**. Using the example of the friend or (adult) child, above, instead of worry being focused on a specific event (travelling abroad) and being contained, we are anxious **all the time** that **'something' might happen to them**. We are not even sure what that might be. It is just a 'feeling', a 'premonition' that something bad *could* happen to them. While we can usually be distracted from, or 'reason away' worries, anxiety persists. **Anxiety** is more likely to **trigger our fear, 'fight or flight' physical response** so that we sense our heart racing, our hands shaking, our palms sweating and our muscles tense. This can make us even more anxious as we now focus on the physical symptoms as signs of illness in ourselves. Thus, while worry can be helpful, prompting us to act, anxiety can 'paralyse' us, with endless thoughts and concerns whirling around our heads of possible (terrible) outcomes and scenarios.

Cancer and depression

One of the difficulties in assessing distress and mood in the context of cancer is that, unsurprisingly, many people with cancer are distressed and low. Distinguishing this from a 'clinical' depression – pervasive overwhelming sadness that is part of a mood disorder – can be very difficult. However, it must be done, otherwise patients are struggling with two illnesses – cancer and depression. This 'clinical' depression is very different from the anguish and sadness people can have with cancer. It is all-encompassing, pervasive, persistent. Enjoyment, even of small things, vanishes – nothing lifts it.

Why is it important to recognise 'clinical' depression and anxiety?

They have a negative impact on quality of life

Generally, if we have moved beyond the concept of 'distress' and are using the term 'depression' or 'anxiety', it means that your distress has not resolved and has instead crystallised into a clinical state, meaning persistent low mood or sadness, lack of enjoyment or interest, negative thinking patterns. The concern is that each of these facets can begin to augment each other, causing the anxiety or depression to take a greater hold.

Depression and anxiety can lead to other problems including cancer-related fatigue

If depression continues to worsen, the reduced motivation, interest and enjoyment can lead to reduced activity and exercise. This, in turn, can cause deconditioning and cancer-related fatigue.

Depression can become a life-threatening illness

While severe clinical depression is very unusual in patients with cancer, there is always the risk that what is initially a relatively mild or moderately severe depression may worsen, bringing with it the incapacity and risks of very severe depression. Early intervention is focused to prevent this deterioration.

What can be done?

Levels 1, 2 'distress' – support and psycho-education

If you look again at the SJH psycho-oncology model (Figure 1), you will see that mild distress may recover with simple techniques such as support from family and friends and your cancer teams – 'normalising' and educating you to give you an understanding of what is happening (psycho-education).

Teresa, a teacher, was a quietly capable mother of five children. Diagnosed with cancer two months previously, she was tearful and upset, feeling that her life had been 'thrown up into the air'; everything was chaotic; nothing was certain. Tense, worried, sleeping poorly, she was further distressed by the fact that she 'couldn't put on a brave face', felt a 'failure' for not 'holding it together'. As a result, her head, in addition to thoughts and fears about cancer, was also filled with self-blame and self-recrimination for being so 'weak' and 'useless' in managing her cancer.

A brief discussion with her cancer nurse, putting her fears in perspective, acknowledging that it was still 'very early' since her cancer diagnosis, that her reaction was normal, to be expected, appropriate, even helpful in prompting her to organise practical support for herself and her family, was enough to settle Teresa's additional distress and self-blame.

If you have more severe distress, this may have transformed into 'clinical' (more severe) anxiety or depression, needing structure treatment. The intervention will depend on how severe this is.

Levels 3, 4 'moderate anxiety or depression' – What can we do when thoughts are making us depressed or anxious?

For more (moderately) severe depression, structured psychological intervention, such as cognitive behaviour therapy, is often helpful. This technique focuses first on helping you to **identify** unhelpful thinking patterns and behaviours and then helping you to **challenge and change** them. It has the added advantage that the skills you use you can continue to apply throughout your life.

When CBT was developed for depression, much of the work was focused on challenging negative thoughts and beliefs. Generally, because depression distorts reality, it was relatively easy to challenge these thoughts – such as 'I am a failure', 'My life is worthless'. The difficulty in cancer, is that some of the 'sad' thoughts are real, **there are bad things happening**. With cancer, therefore, instead of focusing on 'challenging' the thoughts and 'proving they are "true" or "not true"', you may have to accept that yes, these thoughts may be true but **are they helpful?**

Avril was the mother of three young boys. She was 41 when she was told she had breast cancer. While her treatment had been very successful, her doctors would not give her any guarantee that her cancer would not come back. She found herself dwelling on this fact all the time. She thought, 'After all the treatment, pain and suffering that I have been through I still have no guarantee'; 'My cancer might come back and I might die.'

She began to imagine what it would be like to have to go on treatment again and whether she would manage it a second time. She became preoccupied by thoughts of her own death and the impact that would have on her family and friends.

These negative thoughts so occupied her mind that she could not think of anything else. They prevented her from interacting fully with her children, family and friends. She withdrew from many of her activities. Filled with thoughts and images of recurrence, cancer treatment and death, she became desperately sad and low. She lost interest in everything, could enjoy nothing. Night-time was the worst – she would lie awake and these thoughts would whirl round in her head.

Avril's story is an example of the very difficult situations people face after cancer treatment. It shows how potentially realistic but negative thoughts can adversely affect your life and your recovery, through effects on your behaviour and mood.

If we were to simply challenge these thoughts, in the way we normally do in CBT, we might find that they cannot be completely 'ruled out' by the evidence available. Avril is right – her cancer might come back and she might die from it. **But at this moment in time, her cancer is not back, she is physically well.**

So instead we ask the question – *How helpful is it for you to dwell on these distressing, unpleasant thoughts (my cancer might come back and I might die)?*

103

Avril struggled to make a list of 'advantages' and 'disadvantages' of this pattern of thinking. In the 'advantages' column she included making her 'super-alert' to any symptoms, ready to identify any sign that the cancer was back – although she did note that this meant she had spent a lot of time at her doctors having repeated tests. Another advantage was that the constant worry that she might die and leave her family behind meant that she spent as much time as possible with her family, although she noted that this time was 'ruined' by how miserable she felt.

Her list of disadvantages of thinking in this way was long: it made her feel sad; it made her act and feel like she was already dying; it interfered with her ability to enjoy her time; it made her tearful; it dominated conversations with her partner, putting a lot of pressure on their relationship; it stopped her from meeting up with friends... The list continued.

Reflecting in this way allowed Avril to see that **any benefit** gained from thinking in this way **was greatly outweighed by the cost** of thinking this way.

The next step was to try to find **more helpful or useful ways** of thinking about the situation.

Every time the thoughts started for her, Avril decided to say, '*Yes, the cancer might come back, but it might not. Nobody knows what is going to happen in the future, so why waste my time thinking about what might not ever happen. Instead I am going to focus on what I can do to live the best-quality life that I can.*'

It is important to say that many of these interventions and challenges are very difficult. Many are done in the context of a well-established, supportive therapeutic relationship between the patient and their therapist. For some of you reading this in a book, it may be too difficult to undertake on your own, you may need structured CBT with a therapist or referral to the psycho-oncology service – please discuss with your cancer team if unsure.

Level 5 'distress/depression'

This level indicates very severe depression.

Leo was a quiet man in his early 40s. An office worker, he had needed a BMT for cancer. He had recovered well, but had needed to stay on steroids for a very long time. As his steroid dose was reduced, his mood began to drop. While this is not uncommon when steroids are reduced, Leo's mood fell more rapidly and to a much lower level than usual. Over time he became extremely withdrawn, barely able to talk to family and friends. He spent most of the day in bed, not wanting to face the world. He described himself as sad and low. He had lost interest in everything. Nothing gave him pleasure. At times, he felt life was not worth living. He felt utterly hopeless, believed that things were 'never going to improve'. In recent days, he was finding it difficult to eat and drink – he just had no interest. Yet his cancer was cured.

Leo had developed severe depression. He needed anti-depressant medication, together with expert psychological intervention (CBT). His mood gradually improved over the next few weeks. He needed careful follow-up over the next six months but, ultimately, he was discharged from out-patient care and his antidepressant medication was discontinued.

Distress is almost inevitable in response to cancer. If it

persists, or becomes severe, you are likely to need extra, expert help. The key first step is to work out where you may lie on the 'cancer pyramid' and then seek a treatment to match that. As always, I encourage you to discuss this with your cancer team if you are not certain.

9

Cancer and Fatigue

Jean, a 65-year-old married lady, had finished her cancer treatment two years previously. Married to a farmer, she had always been a busy lady, fiercely independent, and proud of her contribution to the farm and her home. She had weathered her cancer diagnosis and treatment quietly. However, since her treatment ended, she had become almost a complete recluse. Permanently exhausted, overcome with fatigue, she rarely left her bed. Even the effort of making her way to the kitchen exhausted her. Previously a proud cook, now she listlessly watched her family making the meals, doing the baking, feeling tired out even by 'peeling and chopping vegetables'. She couldn't explain what had happened to her, feeling mute, helpless and indescribably lost. Her inability to take part in her home and her family were bitter blows for her. Even though her cancer was 'cured', 'gone', she felt that she had been 'robbed', had 'lost everything'.

Referred to psycho-oncology, much of her story had to be told by her partner, as Jean herself was too tired to take part in the interview.

The term '**Cancer-related fatigue**' is an easy phrase to say, and seemingly an easy concept. However, in fact, it represents a very complex set of symptoms and behaviours, with equally complex origins. It is a state that is fostered by a complex mix of thoughts (often 'myths'), behaviours and feelings that interact together, often making your situation even worse.

Almost every patient with cancer has, or has heard of, cancer-related fatigue. Patients view the state with a sense of doom and inevitability, 'the price they pay' for having had cancer. When the psycho-oncology service at SJH was first established, the generally accepted international standard management for cancer-related fatigue was injections of a drug that stimulated blood cells. There was relatively little consideration, and little understanding, of the complex biological, psychological and social factors that combine to augment and perpetuate cancer-related fatigue. Admittedly, it can often be difficult to unravel the various factors that contribute to cancer-related fatigue. However, failure to do so can lead to a debilitating existence for patients with cancer.

Careful work with Jean over the coming weeks and months disentangled the many threads of her story, each needing interventions: her depressed mood; the 'advice' she had so rigorously followed, to 'rest', meaning that she had spent most of her time in bed, ultimately becoming so deconditioned that she was unable to do the simplest of tasks; the realisation that these effects had made her utterly miserable and humiliated, wiping away the final remnants of her determination, motivation and pride.

During cancer treatment, while in 'active' treatment, fatigue is common. The stress of attending the hospital, multiple encounters with staff and other patients, the constant realisation one has cancer, often lead to overwhelming fatigue and exhaustion. And that is before one even considers the effects of the treatments themselves – chemotherapy, radiotherapy and surgery. So, much like the 'tunnel of tests', during the 'tunnel of treatment' patients need to respond to this tiredness and rest appropriately, taking the advice of their cancer team. One word of caution, however – if it is possible to take some exercise, however mild, during this time, this will help to reduce the risk of overwhelming fatigue in the later months. As we are about to discuss, the deconditioning effect of total rest cannot be overestimated.

However, as treatment ends, people, even though often overwhelmed at the end of treatment, will need to consider how to rehabilitate themselves, both physically and mentally. This can be difficult. However, if you do not actively seek to rehabilitate yourself, cancer-related fatigue can develop.

Cancer-related fatigue – interventions

When we first began in psycho-oncology, over 20 years ago, cancer-related fatigue, even months and years after treatment, was regarded as 'inevitable'. Patients referred to Psycho-oncology, unsurprisingly, often felt similarly and were 'indignant' at being referred for psychological assessment – *'I have had cancer – what can you possibly do for me?'*

These views were a combination of stigma and a reluctance to attend for psychological support that was fuelled by the myth that fatigue was an inevitable price of cancer. Yet many of the people referred were often six months, a year, or, in some cases, several years post treatment – 'cancer-free', but still almost completely debilitated by fatigue.

Fatigue is the end-point of many potential pathways – physical and psychological. In this chapter on cancer-related fatigue, we are discussing fatigue where specific physical factors have been excluded and are focusing on the interaction between multiple physical and psychological factors.

Cancer-related fatigue – first, an explanation

Of course, there may be physical causes to explain fatigue – and in the case of cancer and cancer treatments there are many: anaemia (low blood counts); hypothyroidism (under-active thyroid); hypoadrenalism (underactive adrenal gland), to mention a few. Similarly, during (and immediately after) cancer treatment, the treatments themselves can cause fatigue.

In the setting of cancer, and cancer treatment, one must always consider these physical causes first. Close working relationships between departments of surgery, medicine and psychological medicine (psycho-oncology) should mean that patients with cancer are considered from every angle, ensuring that all options are considered.

We are focusing in this chapter on people who are at least six months post treatment. Many of these direct effects have gone (or should have). We must then look at the complex interactions between more enduring medical/physical problems and other behavioural, social or psychological impacts that are contributing to reduced activity (and fatigue) and with which we can help.

Cancer-related fatigue – deconditioning and the impact of failure

Patients with cancer are **inundated with advice**, mainly well-meaning, but very confusing. One recurrent theme, with respect to exercise, is to 'take plenty of rest'. While this can be very helpful advice, especially during active treatment, if continued in the weeks and months after treatment, it can lead to a vicious cycle of deconditioning, an increasing sense of helplessness, demoralisation and humiliation.

Jim, a 43-year-old office worker, had always prided himself on his physical fitness. A runner, he generally ran 10 km daily, averaging 20–30 km at the weekend. He was particularly distressed when he got cancer, feeling that his healthy lifestyle should have prevented it. However, he tackled his cancer treatment energetically, launching himself at every hurdle, impatient to get back to work and fitness.

At the end of this treatment, however, he was utterly exhausted. Strictly following the advice he had been given by many, he continued to rest for long periods of the day, believing that this would eventually cause his fatigue to 'lift'. He increasingly felt unable to face even the simplest of tasks, spending much of his time in bed or on the couch downstairs.

Over the following months, he felt himself getting worse. Even climbing the stairs left him exhausted and breathless. He lay on the couch, thinking of the long distances he used to run effortlessly, and felt angry and upset.

One day, he thought to himself, 'This is ridiculous. The doctors

111

have said I am physically fine. I am going out to run.' He threw aside the blankets, put on his running shoes and left the house. Initially delighted to be outside and running, he felt euphoric. 'This is it – I am back!' However, within a short distance, he became breathless and exhausted and had to rest. He made his way home dejected. The next day he felt worse. Every muscle ached. He could barely move. He spent a week recovering, carefully resting. A week later, he tried again – the same thing happened. He repeated this process a few times over the next few months, finally giving up in despair. All his efforts had confirmed for him his worst fear – he would never be the same again. Even though the cancer was gone, its effects would be there forever. He was 'a ruined man'.

Eventually, he was referred to the Psycho-oncology service, where his story was recognised as a typical story of cancer-related fatigue. Explaining to Jim the factors discussed below was the first step in helping him to recognise what was happening. Building a structured exercise programme, supporting him with his goals and managing his fears and expectations helped him to slowly regain his previous levels of activity and fitness, including returning to running. One factor that was most helpful to Jim was applying his strategies for training as an athlete to his strategies for dealing with his cancer-related fatigue.

Jim's story is not unusual. Starting from a baseline of no activity, told their cancer is 'cured', people suddenly hurl themselves into activity they would previously have considered 'easy'. Completely deconditioned, their body just simply cannot respond. Often repeated a few times, this 'failure' confirms to the person their belief that 'all is lost'. Even though they are 'cancer-free', cancer has 'robbed them of their future'. Eventually, demoralised and defeated, they stop trying.

Many patients who are, understandably, upset and unnerved by these experiences, find it very difficult to consider their situation objectively. Their experience and their fatigue make it very difficult to engage with even the simplest of alternative explanations. Yet, as discussed throughout this book, **understanding the roots of the problem** is the first step to taking control, the first step to 'rooting out' the roots and moving to an alternative, better place.

Cancer-related fatigue is, at least in part (the part the psycho-oncology can work with), the interaction between the deconditioning effect of treatment, the unhelpful impact of further 'resting', ill-advised attempts to return suddenly to previous levels of activity, unhelpful 'beliefs' that result from these experiences and the emotional impact leading to demoralisation, distress and ultimately withdrawal.

Deconditioning

Deconditioning is the 'first' step in this spiral. Understanding exactly what deconditioning is, and just how bad it can be – as well as realising it is an inevitable but **reversible** effect of what you have been through – is the first step to tackle.

For our muscles to work properly, for the complex brain-body system that helps us all to function, we must use our muscles, keep our balance, regularly. When we are well, we do not even think about this. We (mainly!) jump out of bed (a complex manoeuvre, requiring muscle strength, co-ordination, activation of our sympathetic nervous system, stimulation of our baroreceptors), walk, sit, stand and move all day. We 'exercise' without even thinking about it.

If we do not exercise, sit, stand or walk, our muscles rapidly decay. They 'decondition' due to lack of use. The situation is then often worsened by what you experience when you try to stand up to walk – feeling weak, dizzy, 'woozy', nauseated – so that you presume there is something seriously wrong and retreat to the safety of your bed. And so, the cycle of inactivity, deconditioning, inactivity, de-moralisation begins.

Of course, most people do not 'give up' that quickly. They think back to their previous levels of fitness, they tell them-selves they are 'cured', they argue it is 'mind over matter' and, like Jim, they hurl themselves into action – with, like Jim, often very disappointing results.

Any person wanting to go up a whole flight of stairs generally uses each step – perhaps every two steps if athletic and in a hurry. But certainly, no one considers going from the bottom to the top in one leap. But this is what Jim was doing. Starting at the bottom and attempting to get straight to the top without any step in between – inevitably doomed to failure. What he must recognise is that he is now on the bottom step with respect to his fitness, a difficult admission for someone with Jim's previous level of fitness, but a true one. He needs to devise a rehabilitation programme that will allow him to gradually increase his level of fitness, starting at a level way below his normal one, and slowly building up.

Practical tips for a physical rehabilitation programme

Based on this information you can begin to devise your own rehabilitation programme. Those of you who are engaged in sport will understand better the concept of training and slowly increasing ability, step by step. It is a little more difficult, perhaps, without experience of sport. Yet the principles are the same.

- It may be enough to develop this programme on your own – make sure to write out your plans with an achievable target for each week – this will depend on your starting point. If you make the target too difficult you will not be able to complete it and this will further fuel your sense of dejection. Choose an initial target that is difficult but achievable for you.
- Ideally enlist the help of a family member or friend.
- Ask your physiotherapist for help if necessary.
- Remember to include very specific targets.
- Acknowledge every milestone or target that you reach.
- Reward yourself – be kind!

Cancer-related fatigue – other things to consider – thoughts, behaviours, feelings – the vicious cycle

So far in this chapter, we have concentrated on behaviours – physical activity and deconditioning. As you will have seen from other chapters, however, things rarely occur in isolation. Often, the behaviour, the lack of exercise and sense of fatigue, is caused by the interactions between those behaviours, your thoughts and your feelings.

Thoughts and fatigue

We have previously discussed 'myths' about cancer. There are, of course, many similar 'myths' about cancer-related fatigue. One of these myths is the belief that energy levels will have been damaged forever because of cancer or its treatment. This is not the case. But, if you believe this, the inevitable response, the associated behaviour is to sleep frequently during the day and stop almost all activities. This can cause a 'perfect storm' as ceasing activity and poor sleep patterns can actually worsen fatigue

It is important to recognise, however, that cancer-related fatigue is neither inevitable nor incurable. Taking the simple steps discussed above will allow you to begin to reclaim your previous levels of activity and fitness. Sometimes, the lack of success, the enforced dependence can lead to depressed mood, self-blame, humiliation, anger and shame. Occasionally, mood can become so low that it may need separate treatment. If this happens, you will need to discuss this with your cancer team. The most important step, however, is to recognise the problem and begin to address it to allow yourself to move towards recovery.

10

Cancer and Sleep, Intimacy, Body Image, Infertility and Other Issues

Difficulty with sleep (insomnia) is one of the most common problems during and after cancer treatment. Almost everyone with cancer will have sleep difficulty at some point. Many people, however, have difficulty with sleep **before** they ever had cancer. Nonetheless, cancer and its many treatments can make sleep difficulties significantly worse.

Difficulties with sleep may include problems getting to sleep (taking more than 30 minutes); staying asleep (waking during the night and finding it difficult to get back to sleep); or waking up too early. Saying someone has 'insomnia' is simply saying they have difficulty sleeping. Identifying potential causes and remedying them can be very difficult.

Conor, finished with his cancer treatment, still felt exhausted. He climbed into bed every night, desperate for sleep. Sometimes he fell asleep for an hour or two, but was always awake again by 1 o'clock. In the quiet of the night his mind raced with worrying thoughts, his heart racing, his muscles tense. He tossed and turned, willing himself to sleep. He watched the minutes tick by on the clock, becoming more and more distressed, knowing he would be exhausted again the next day. Soon he began to stay in bed, reluctant to face the day. He spent much of his days resting, napping in the afternoons to 'compensate' for his poor sleep at night-time.

This is an example of sleep being disrupted by the worry of cancer, further worsened by Conor's understandable responses to the lack of sleep – daytime naps. This sets up a vicious cycle where daytime naps make night-time sleeping worse.

How does cancer affect sleep?

There are many different ways that cancer can affect sleep. There is no point in simply saying, 'This person can't sleep because they have cancer.' The question is – in what way is cancer contributing to the insomnia?

Probably the first, most important question is 'Were you a poor sleeper before you had cancer?' If the answer is 'yes', it is unsurprising that the stress of cancer and its treatment have made this worse. A careful look at what is actually happening, each part of your sleep routine, may help to devise strategies to improve things.

Possible links between cancer and insomnia include:

- Stress and worry about cancer.
- Recurrent time staying in hospital, in noisy wards, where people are woken up for medication and food and where no one sleeps well.
- Intermittent use of sleeping tablets, especially when in hospital. Sleeping tablets disrupt normal sleep patterns

and may therefore cause difficulty when they are with-drawn at home.

- Medications' side-effects. Some medications cause insomnia.
- Pain – no one can sleep properly if they are in pain.
- Hot flushes also interfere with sleep.
- Alcohol. While alcohol may initially help to get off to sleep, ultimately, like sleeping tablets, it can interfere with sleep quality and disrupts sleep.
- Other night-time disruptions, for example, having to get up to go to the toilet, being attached to night-time drug infusions or feeds.

Other ways in which cancer worsens insomnia are that the fatigue and exhaustion that can accompany cancer or cancer treatment may cause you to feel tired and sleepy during the day. This can, understandably, lead you to:

- take prolonged daytime naps, which disrupt night-time sleep
- spend prolonged periods in bed, reducing daytime exercise
- drink extra caffeine to try to give yourself 'energy', which disrupts night-time sleep.

Managing cancer-related insomnia

You can already see just how complex the 'simple' behaviour of sleeping is, and how many things can affect it.

There are many excellent guidebooks on managing insomnia (see Appendix). These give general advice about sleep-promoting behaviours and how to maximise sleep.

Managing specific issues in the context of cancer that keep you from sleep

Stress and worry about cancer

This is perhaps the biggest challenge for patients with cancer and insomnia. Many patients are prone to anxious and sad thoughts after cancer diagnosis and treatment. Often these thoughts include fears about the cancer coming back, regrets, guilt or sadness. Added to this is the worry of not sleeping. Fears and concerns that could be dismissed, or seem much less, in the cold light of day can feel 'out of control' in the loneliness of the night. As patients often say, *'Nothing is as bad as it seems at four o'clock in the morning'.*

The difficulty is that these general anxious thoughts then fuel the concerns about not sleeping, leading to poor sleep, further anxiety and another vicious circle. Tackling some of the general cancer myths and thinking behaviours means that you can refer back to this if these anxieties start to crowd into your mind as you are falling asleep. Another strategy, below, is to 'put your day to bed before you put yourself to bed'.

Put your day to bed before you put yourself to bed

It can be helpful, as suggested by sleep experts such as Charles Morin and Colin Espie, to set aside time to 'put your thoughts to rest' at the end of your day, well before sleep, as part of your night-time routine. (This is a version of 'worry time' –

setting time aside each day for your worries). Plan for the next day, using pen and paper. Later in the evening, remind yourself that you have dealt with the day, and will face new tasks the next day. If thoughts creep in, say to yourself you will add them to your list in the morning – you have dealt with them already.

Worry time

A variant of putting your day to bed is setting aside time to worry. Some people are inveterate 'worriers' – really a form of generalised anxiety disorder. They often justify their worry on the basis that it allows them to be prepared for every eventuality. Setting aside 15–30 minutes every evening (early) when you can worry as much as you like means that if you start to worry at other times, you say to yourself, 'I will worry about that later.'

Other strategies

Rather than lying in bed, focused on not sleeping, worrying about every passing minute that you have not slept, instead focus on staying awake! Focus on relaxing, being 'grateful' for the time to relax and rejuvenate, keep your eyes open and gratefully allow them to slowly droop, if and when it happens.

Medications

Medications are generally, in the long-term, unhelpful with respect to sleep. Avoid sleeping tablets if possible. They ultimately disrupt normal sleep patterns. Similarly, try to avoid using alcohol and caffeine – especially in the evening time. Some medications disrupt sleep. Review your medication list with your team.

Exercise and daytime naps

Review your exercise during the day. Prolonged periods in bed during the daytime and, particularly, daytime naps, will interfere with your ability to sleep at night. Try to slowly reduce your nap times. Schedule other activities for when you normally nap – for example, meeting a friend or going for a walk.

Cancer – intimacy and body image

For many people after cancer treatment, resuming an intimate relationship including a sexual relationship can seem a bridge too far. Many feel that their body has been 'ravaged' by their cancer treatment. For some, this is visible to everyone, as in, for example, the person who has had extensive facial surgery. For others, it is not immediately visible, but the person is acutely aware of a change in their shape (for example, after a mastectomy) or body function (those who have had bowel surgery and now have a bowel 'bag'). Sometimes the change is hardly visible at all – but for the person affected the impact is huge. This is, perhaps, the most important point. It is the meaning for you, the person who has had the treatment, that is key. These impacts happen even if people have not had surgery – chemotherapy causing hair loss with regrowth of 'curly' instead of 'straight' hair; altered gait due to nerve damage. The central factor is how the impact of these changes are felt, experienced, interpreted and managed by **you**, the person to whom they have happened. Because before you can take the first brave step to entrusting yourself in a close, physically intimate relationship with someone else, you must feel comfortable with yourself – not always easy when you have just survived cancer treatment.

Feeling comfortable with yourself

Tommy was a bright outgoing 22-year-old, working in a public setting, when he developed a large tumour growing behind his nose. Prior to his surgery, he socialised regularly, played soccer with some of his old college friends weekly, ran with a local group twice a week, went to the pub every weekend. Although he did not have a 'steady' partner, he had several girlfriends.

Tommy's facial surgery left him very changed physically. He had a long scar down the side of his face and he had lost most of his nose, some teeth, and the roof of his mouth due to surgery. While his cancer was now 'gone', he had difficulty eating and drinking and his speech was difficult to understand.

Tommy was devastated. For the first few days after surgery, he did not want to even leave his hospital room. Going home to his (rural) town seemed an impossible task. His head was full of thoughts such as 'I am ugly', 'I can't talk or eat properly', 'No one will want to be with me', 'People will stare when they see me'. Tommy felt sad, anxious, depressed, disappointed, angry and hurt about what had happened to him. He was very self-conscious about his appearance, describing himself as having a 'Jekyll and Hyde' appearance. He began to feel tense and on edge most of the time. He developed headaches, constant 'palpitations' and was unable to sleep. He avoided his friends, refusing to let them visit him, convinced they would reject him if they met him. He spent most of his time alone, initially in his hospital room, later in his home. He became constantly tired and fatigued, unable to do any of the physical exercise he used to love to do.

While Tommy's story is a dramatic one, even people with less invasive treatment describe these feelings of isolation, fear, embarrassment and distress. For Tommy, some of what he described was true, and had to be acknowledged. He had had significant facial surgery with significant changes in his appearance. What he had to decide now was whether he would allow this to rule his life. How helpful was it to him to focus on these thoughts, to have them direct his behaviour in this way? It was a very big step for Tommy, and took enormous courage, for him to accept that yes, his appearance had changed and yes, strangers, or even friends meeting him again for the first time after surgery might stare, or even make a totally unhelpful comment. But he was still the same person he had always been – with the same sense of fun and humour, the energy and interest in sports and fitness and the fondness for going to his local pub (although he admitted that 'downing the pints' did not have quite the same allure as before). He had to accept that people that he cared about, who genuinely cared about him, would look beyond his changed appearance. Those who didn't, he would have to leave behind. He described this as 'one of the gifts of his cancer' – the freedom to choose – to only have in his life those people who made him feel better, not worse – *'I never waste time now with those that I regard as "toxic" people – life is just too short.'*

Once Tommy had thought things through, made careful plans about whom he would meet and share his vulnerable self with, his life began to change. It was almost a military exercise, much like the rehabilitation programme for cancer fatigue. He carefully selected those friends he most trusted, slowly enlarging his circle. He went back to graded exercise, initially running with one or two friends, again slowly enlarging the circle, the distance and the speed. As he changed his thoughts and his behaviours, his feelings and experiences changed too. The tense, heavy feeling in his chest began to lift, his palpitations stopped and his sleep improved. Of course, he had many setbacks along the way – insensitive people who said the 'wrong thing'; people who stared or walked away. Friends who rejected him. But he had developed strategies to deal with that and he reminded himself constantly that his strength needed to come from himself first, and he would allow nothing and no one to rob him of that.

Feeling comfortable with yourself
– beyond Tommy's story

Tommy's story is, of course, an extreme one. But the same principles apply to anyone who feels that their 'bodily integrity', their 'sense of wholeness' has been disrupted by cancer and its treatment. It is not always due to surgery. It may not even be apparent or visible to anyone else. It is about looking at how one is going to manage what is often a very difficult reality, and deciding what thoughts and behaviours, what responses are going to be best for you.

Helen was 19 when she needed a bone-marrow transplant for cancer. Young and otherwise healthy, she did 'well'. However, she needed to remain on high-dose steroids for months after her treatment. And this devastated her in ways she had not even considered. Tall, slim and athletic, with excellent skin, she had always been self-assured about her appearance, mixing easily with friends and strangers.

Now, having taken high-dose steroids for six months she felt like 'an alien from outer space, an enormous blob'. She had gained 15 kg in weight, her hair had thinned to the point of being almost invisible, her face was covered in acne, the muscles in her arms and thighs had vanished while her core had 'swelled' so that she felt like a 'lemon on sticks'. The skin on her tummy had become weak and lax and she had bright purple marks across her lower tummy that had never been there before.

Hugely self-conscious and fragile after her treatment, these seemed like hurdles she just could not overcome. Managing people that she met was just too difficult.

Like many other stories, Helen's initial response was to hide herself away. However, this led to further distress and despair. Starved of the friendships and activities that normally sustained her, she despaired of ever returning to life.

For Helen, understanding that many people on long-term steroids suffer in this way was an important first step in beginning to address her situation. Then, focusing on what she **could** do, what she **could** reclaim, identifying friends who were supportive without being judgemental was crucial. Ultimately, Helen's steroids were reduced and stopped, and many of the side-effects melted away. But Helen, by then, had already 'reclaimed' two years of her life and, in her own words, had 'learned lessons about managing others' that she had never even considered before.

Feeling comfortable about yourself – close, intimate and sexual relationships

Sarah's and Susan's stories:

Sarah was a 28-year-old woman when she got breast cancer. She had been in a relationship with Susan for the previous ten years and they were a very close couple. Sarah, however, had been devastated by her cancer diagnosis. Needing a mastectomy, radiotherapy and chemotherapy, she felt her appearance had been utterly changed by her cancer treatment. She thought her appearance 'repulsive', 'revolting' and 'totally unattractive'. She could not accept that **anyone**, not even her beloved Susan could see her in any other way.

Upset, distressed, humiliated and embarrassed, she began to hide her appearance from Susan – locking her out of the bedroom when she was getting undressed, quickly hiding herself from her, covering herself up, snapping angrily at her on the occasions when Susan tried to touch her or even open a conversation about how she looked or how she felt about her.

Eventually, Susan began to withdraw, avoiding looking at Sarah, remaining resolutely far away from her on her side of the bed. This confirmed for Sarah that she had been correct – she was deeply repulsive, deformed and unattractive. Her sense of devastation – and the silence between herself and Susan grew.

Susan was distraught. She had suffered hugely watching Sarah endure endless treatments. She was in awe of her dignity and bravery. She was so relieved for her that she had been 'cured', although still fearful of what the future might bring. To her, she was even more attractive and endearing – a symbol of courage and endurance. But she felt hugely hurt by what she felt was *constant rejection by Sarah. She could do nothing right. Every time she tried to even discuss what was happening, Sarah was angry and rejecting. Eventually, she decided that the best course of action was to do nothing. Now she herself was afraid she would never be able to have a sexual relationship – she felt too unsure of herself to even consider it.*

These accounts are so common for relationships in cancer – not just for intimate sexual relationships, but for all inter- actions – people who are close being overwhelmed by unhelpful thoughts and feelings that drive them even further apart, unable to talk to each other to try to undo the tangles of miscommunication.

For Sarah to have any intimate relationships with Susan, she needed first to be comfortable with herself. It seemed cruel to her that having had to endure her cancer treatment, she now had to have very difficult conversations with herself about the impact of that treatment on her body and her life – an example of the very difficult situations people can find themselves in after cancer treatment.

Sarah had several choices. She could continue as she was – which was making her miserable and she did not want to do so. She could challenge whether or not she was correct in saying that she was now 'repulsive'. Or she could accept that these were very unhelpful thoughts for her, that they were affecting her behaviour and her relationship with Susan in ways that were 'robbing' her of her life. She had to 'take a risk' with Susan.

They attended specific therapy sessions together. In the safety of those sessions they were able to discuss the impact of what had happened on them both. Sarah had not considered the impact of what had happened on Susan. For the first time she saw how hurt, bewildered and isolated Susan felt. Susan, in turn, was hugely supportive and tender to Sarah, and Sarah saw that she did not find her repulsive – she needed and wanted her more than ever.

These are very difficult situations. Sarah and Susan needed specific psychological sessions in a 'safe' space with an expert to manage their situation. For some of you reading this book, you may need the same. For others (and your partners), we hope that by reading about these reactions, informing yourself, **understanding** what is happening for everyone may allow you to make choices, to change your behaviour enough to allow you to take the first brave step back into an intimate relationship after cancer. If you are not sure, please discuss with your cancer team.

Infertility

It is hard, almost impossible, to describe the sense of devastation people describe on learning they are infertile following cancer treatment. People, of course, experience it in differing ways.

Having her own children had always been a driving wish for Michelle. Third child in a large family, her dream was to have her own large family of children – 'at least six', she told me. Working in childcare, her love of children had not dimmed. With a steady partner, saving for their own home, she had felt life was with her every step of the way. Until cancer struck. She had endured six years of cancer treatment. Each time she thought she had recovered, her cancer returned. She had spent a total of six months in Intensive Care, 'nearly died' three times. Now, finally, at home, 'cancer-free', she was barely strong enough to stand for more than five minutes. She could not even contemplate returning to her work and was struggling in her relationships.

She spent 12 months working hard at a rehabilitation programme to address physical, psychological and social factors. It had been extremely difficult – but she had persisted. Her partner supported her throughout. At the end of that time, she felt well. She was finally in a position to look at where she was with respect to having children. And her devastation hit all over again as the enormous realisation about the impact of infertility hit her. She railed, wailed, wept at her fate. 'Life is too cruel.' She withdrew into herself, refused to meet friends, isolated herself at home, spent all her time focused on the huge loss of not being able to have children. Sessions with the Psychological Medicine Service were curtailed by her extreme distress. It was not possible to do anything but listen and support her.

Slowly, however, very slowly, as she had done in every other area of her recovery, she began to strategise and make plans about her position. She spoke to her partner who was supportive of whatever plans she made. She consulted experts about IVF (in vitro fertilisation) and surrogacy. And she put those plans in place. She even began to accept that she might never have children of her own – and began to talk of adoption.

Ultimately, Michelle did have, not one, but three, biological children. Hearing that news was a moment of joy shared by everyone who had been involved in her care – a testament to human perseverance in the face of reality and a source of inspiration for every health-care worker that had been involved in her care – moments that have a worth and an impact that last forever and are beyond measure.

However, this, of course, is not the reality for many patients. But what Michelle had done, before she had her children, was to somehow accept what was for her a bitter and harsh reality and make plans to live her life around that reality, to look at what she did have and build on that.

Managing intimacy, infertility, view of self - what is the common theme?

Anyone reading each of these patient stories will, I think, see common themes, even though the impact of each of these situations will be very different, very individualised. These themes are, as always, best summarised by one of my patients:

'For me, it was the ability to stand back from the "trap" of being swallowed up, engulfed by the focus on the darkness of what had happened to me; to instead shine a light on what was possible, letting go of the hurt and anger at what I could not have, building on what I could do, following a path towards a life that was fulfilling for me.'

This is a 'big ask'. And whether or not you can even contemplate it, depends on many things, the first of which is 'where you are' in your cancer treatment. It really is only possible to consider these more complex, enduring problems when, like Michelle, you have recovered your physical, psychological and emotional strength. If you have, then please consider them. If this text is not enough, please talk to your cancer team about a referral to psycho-oncology, as some of these struggles are just too difficult to manage on your own. The greatest sign of strength is knowing when to ask for help.

Section IV

LIFE AFTER CANCER

11

When Treatment Ends – When Rehabilitation Starts

In earlier chapters we discussed how devastating a diagnosis of cancer can be for patients and for their families. We have seen how they 'make it through' the 'tunnel of tests' – often metaphorically 'closing their eyes', 'gritting their teeth'. Often they adopt a similar approach to their treatment, treating it as a 'tunnel of treatment' – 'shutting everything out' to 'make it through the treatment', to 'get back to their old life when they can be themselves again'. They literally count the days and months to when their treatment will end. It is marked on the calendar (in reality or in their head), for them, for their families and friends, as their day of 'freedom', the day when their lives start again, a day of celebration.

Instead of being a time of joy and celebration, many of our patients have highlighted that this time – the 'end of treatment' – is the worst time for them. For these patients, the sense of desolation, despondency and despair they experience is particularly galling. They feel they have 'done everything right', 'taken it on the chin', 'got to the end' and they are utterly desolated when they find that they do not feel wonderful, relieved, victorious. Instead, they feel exhausted, demoralised and afraid.

Many have said that if they had only known what to expect, the sense of desolation, disappointment and despair might not have been so overwhelming. And they might have been able to plan better, to anticipate.

Being 'back to myself'

I have a particular aversion to the concept that one is 'going back' anywhere. It is not possible, for anyone, ever, to go backwards in time. It is not, therefore, a very helpful goal, especially for someone exhausted and deconditioned after difficult cancer treatment. In fact, I would say it is a particularly unhelpful goal. You will be going **forward**. You will still be you – but a you that has been through a difficult diagnosis and treatment, with the life experience of all that that has brought. Interestingly, some people turn the experience around and use the experience to **never** 'go back' to how they were pre-cancer.

Transitioning into the outside world

It is an irony that, for some, having railed against the world of active cancer treatment for so long, now that the time has come to leave it, they become full of fear, reluctant to leave. Understandably, they fear losing the support, the 'safety' of the cancer unit, where an expert is on hand at all times to see them and reassure them.

As always, the first step is to acknowledge that this is a reasonable view. Many people experience it. It is also a reassuring sign that you are keen to make sure that you are well, that you are doing everything you can to protect yourself.

Leaving the active treatment centre, and moving into the outside world is a real sign of progress. Your team will have thought carefully before making the decision to allow you to leave.

Some words of preparation

Having spent weeks or months cocooned in a slow, quiet, controlled environment (especially if you have been an in-patient), with a tightly controlled timetable of tests, treatments and reviews, it can be truly shocking just to step out of the hospital door and into a busy, loud, thronged street with people and cars rushing past at what seems like 'breakneck' speed. People often feel bewildered and overwhelmed. Add to that the fact that they are often, themselves, still weak and under-powered compared to their baseline, and it can make it distressing and demoralising. Be aware – this was the world you lived in. You were part of it and moved at that speed and urgency right up until you became ill. Ironically, you may decide that you never again want to live in that way – but that is a discussion in a different chapter and for a later time. For now, recognise that this is a normal reaction. You may feel overwhelmed, protective of yourself, afraid of being knocked over, having someone cough in your face. Plan with your family and friends how you will get to your destination, accept help to get to your car or transport.

Getting home

People who have had to spend time as an in-patient for treatment often dream about 'getting home'. They see themselves striding through their front door (as they were before they became ill), grabbing their children, wrestling with the dog, chasing their cat, mowing the lawn, preparing dinner for ten people. They rarely consider the reality. You will reach home exhausted, deconditioned, shaken by your experience. Yes, you will be home and yes, that is wonderful, **but** you need to be kind to yourself and recognise that you just will not be at your baseline on day one. The achievement will be getting in the front door and sitting on the couch listening to the excitement of everyone else.

It would, perhaps, be easier to understand if one could see a broken leg in a plaster – everyone would then automatically take account of the fact that you are still recovering. But you do not have many visible external signs – so you need to remind yourself and everyone else that while, yes, you are home and that is wonderful progress, you are still recovering.

This is important to consider because one of the most disappointing and demoralising experiences that patients describe is pinning all their hopes on their 'return home' and then finding it is so different from where they were. Knowing in advance, congratulating themselves on getting home, and managing to stay upright for an afternoon, is a huge achievement and a wonderful first step in recovery after treatment. Making sure your family and friends also know will help you (and them) to manage the transition.

Longer-term effects of cancer treatments – 'home' but not 'out'

For many patients, cancer treatment and effects last for longer than they had ever anticipated. Some of you, especially after

BMT, may need to stay on long-term drugs to stop your body from rejecting new cells. These can have side-effects that persist. The rehabilitation of your body, improving your muscles, overcoming fatigue takes time. These are discussed in specific chapters dedicated to long-term effects of cancer.

Ultimately, your plan is to move steadily forward into your life, away from hospital, to 'reclaim' your life, up to your baseline or even beyond it.

A closer look at the 'end of treatment'

Geraldine could not stop crying. Day and night, she sobbed until she couldn't cry any more. Aged 43, the mother of two children, she had found her treatment for breast cancer very difficult. Radiation, surgery and chemotherapy, she had had them all. The only thing that had kept her going was the 'magic' date of 20 September – the day her treatment would end. Her friends and family had all counted down the days with her.

Now, two weeks after that date, she was devastated. Exhausted, demoralised, she could barely make a cup of tea. Everyone said to her, 'You must be delighted your cancer is cured.' She felt like screaming. Only now could she really consider the impact of what had happened to her – the fear, the possibility of her death. It was a nightmare.

She was so tired she could barely move. And, suddenly, all the support she had had was melting away. People felt she could manage – 'Wasn't her treatment finished now?' Yet she had never felt more in need of help.

Added to this was her feeling of guilt. She should be grateful, thankful to her treating team, grateful to her friends and family for support – when what she actually felt was tired, angry, upset and, above all, cheated of her life. She had not 'returned to herself'. This anxious, dejected, exhausted person was not the busy, energetic mother-of-two that she had been.

And finally, there was that fear, the tiny voice in her head that kept repeating, 'What if it's not gone? What if it's back? How can you be sure?'

Her weekly trips to the Day Ward – previously seen as a 'life sentence' – she now missed hugely. With no one to check with, every ache and pain she had felt like a warning sign of her cancer back again.

Geraldine felt truly 'robbed' – all her hopes had been pinned on the end of treatment. And now she felt worse than ever.

Geraldine's story is a very typical one. The end of treatment does mark an important milestone for anyone with cancer. You have made it to the end of treatment. You have been able to take whatever treatment was necessary to manage your cancer. And when you look at what has been described in earlier chapters and what you had to go through to get here, that truly is a wonderful achievement. But the end of treatment also brings its own challenges, new different challenges. Huge progress? Yes, absolutely. But there are still steps to complete, challenges to be met, to allow you to reclaim your life fully as you exit from the 'rollercoaster' that is cancer treatment.

'Knowledge is power' – know in advance

As with so many examples in cancer care, knowing what to expect in advance is generally helpful. One of the things that most upsets patients about how they feel at the end of treatment is their sense of being 'cheated' or 'robbed'. They had placed all their hopes on being 'back to themselves', only to find they feel worse. Knowing in advance that often you will feel (much) worse gives you back a sense of control – it is what you expected. Furthermore, it also allows you to put in place **practical strategies** to make that period less difficult, discussed in the following sections.

Family and friends – network of support

Many people offer to help immediately when someone is diagnosed with cancer. Kind and concerned, they offer all types of help – doing the shopping, cooking meals, doing school runs. These are all essential, practical supports for someone going through cancer treatment. However, even for the best-intentioned person, help is often time-limited. And many people regard the 'end of treatment' as when they can begin to withdraw their support. This is true for family as well as friends. Yet the end of treatment is when even more support is needed.

Patients with cancer need the same, if not more, support, as they finish their exhausting, gruelling cancer treatment. Many are exhausted, sore, tired, trying, in some cases, to manage difficulties in eating, drinking, speaking, the effect on their body image or shape. For others, it is also the first time that they really get a chance to sit back and look at what has happened. Until now, they have been on 'the conveyor belt of cancer treatment'. Now it has stopped. They have come off the end. And they get to look at where they have been – often a scary place.

So you need to tell your family and friends that, when treatment ends, you are starting the 'recovery' or 'rehabilitation' phase – and that will take another six to twelve months. During that time, you will be doing many things to get yourself back into better physical and mental shape, but you will need ongoing support with food, car runs, housework, shopping or whatever is needed, until you get to the end of that phase. If the time is less than six to twelve months, that is wonderful. But better to err on the longer side. For those of you (many) who feel guilty about asking for these supports, please look on it as an investment. Either you are reaping the rewards of investments you have previously made helping others or they are making an investment in you, which you will be glad to 'pay back' when fully recovered.

Make a plan – a rehabilitation package – some suggestions

- Plan a **'rehabilitation package'** for yourself for when your cancer treatment ends. Much of the information you need for this has been discussed within this book.
- Ideally, plan this at the start of your treatment, or as soon as possible, while you still feel well enough to plan and strategise.
- Involve your support network of family and friends.
- Consider physical, mental and social wellbeing.
  - Physical wellbeing interventions will include approaches to your food, exercise and sleep habits.
  - Mental wellbeing is, of course, absolutely linked with your physical wellbeing. It will also include ways to

manage fears of recurrence; the 'pains and aches that bother you as you try to get back to "normal"'. Tackling the 'myths' – 'I should be more grateful', 'I should be more delighted' – is also important.

○ Social wellbeing supports both mental and physical wellbeing. Adapt this to what you enjoy. In the early stages it may simply be a phone call or a daily text message exchange. Explain in advance to well-meaning kind friends that you may not be available for phone calls or even texts. Be clear that, despite this, you are aware of, and grateful for, the support (if that is the case).

End of treatment challenges – worry and uncertainty

Fear of recurrence – 'My cancer will come back'

A Greek legend tells the story of Damocles, servant to the King of Syracuse, Sicily. Damocles often said that his king was a great man and lucky to have such power. One day the king, hearing this for yet another time, asked Damocles to trade places with him and be king for one day. Damocles was delighted. He thoroughly enjoyed all the luxuries that came with being a king. All was going well until the evening. Damocles suddenly noticed, hanging directly above his head, by a single horse's hair, a long, evil, sharp sword. He could not relax or enjoy anything from that moment onwards, constantly worrying that the sword might drop and kill him.

He asked the king to remove it. But the king told him that being a king meant he had to live with threat and fear at all times. Damocles immediately swapped back into his servant's life and never again asked to be king.

The king had taught Damocles that the role of king brought with it constant danger – at any moment he is in danger of being assassinated. The king, growing up with this threat, had learned to live with it. But, for Damocles, who suddenly experienced it, it was overwhelming.

How does 'the sword of Damocles' apply to someone with cancer?

The truth is that we all live with a 'sword of Damocles' over our head. We are all going to die. But, generally, we manage to 'forget' about it and focus on our lives instead. We think that 'bad things will happen to someone else'. These beliefs are often further strengthened by the 'rules for living' we heard about earlier: 'I lead a very healthy life; I am a good person – it won't happen to me.' This is an example of bias – we lean towards the good things. It is probably a very useful strategy as it allows us to lead our lives, taking (some) risks, not remaining in our houses, too frightened to leave.

Having cancer overturns all that. You now know that **bad things happen to good people – for no apparent reason**. Cancer forces people to stare their own mortality in the face – a very frightening experience. People feel **vulnerable, afraid** and **uncertain**. For many people, this sense of uncertainty slowly moves to the back of their mind. Time is a great healer. As the days, weeks and months go by, and they are well, people become more confident, less fearful. Yes, there are times when the worries about cancer and the future resurface, for example 'check-ups' and hospital appointments, but generally people begin to return to life.

However, there are some who just cannot take their eyes away from that metaphorical sword. They are constantly thinking about their cancer coming back, getting worse – 'Why me?' 'Will my cancer come back?' 'Has my cancer gone completely?'

It had taken Linda eight months to agree to a referral to psycho-oncology. She still felt irritation and unease at being there. Wasn't it enough that she had had cancer? And had had so much treatment? Yet she knew that things weren't right for her. Told eight months previously that she was 'cured', her cancer was 'gone', she had not been able to return to any sort of life. She spent most of her days waiting for her next medical appointment, her questions ready, waiting to be reassured that her cancer was not back. Every ache, every pain started her into a spiral of dread and despair, believing her cancer had returned. She had even stopped leaving the house. The last time she left she had noticed her breathing more 'noisy' than usual, and imagined her cancer had moved to her lungs, making her even more anxious and her breathing worse. Now she stayed within the four walls of her small apartment, where she spent most days in her chair, noticing every twinge and ache, taken over by the fears, thoughts and images these aches brought with them.

Until she began to discuss these fears at her psycho-oncology appointment, she had not even noticed how awful these images were – images of her death, her dying, her funeral, her body ravaged by disease, her hair falling out (again). It was true what the psychologist said. Even the healthiest of people would become distressed if they continually had those thoughts and images.

Unable to eat, unable to exercise, her physical health had deteriorated. She could now barely move around the apartment without feeling weak. Her world had shrunk. And yet her doctors could find no physical abnormality. With no other focus, her only focus was on her physical sensations, her (awful) images. She knew with certainty her cancer must be back – what else could explain how weak she was, how awful she felt? 'They just hadn't found it yet.'

Some patients finish their cancer treatment, put that 'episode' in their lives behind them and move forward, never considering it again. Most, however, live with the impact of the diagnosis and their treatment. For some, like Linda, the impact continues to have catastrophic effects. Having previously lived with 'certainty', they now know that cancer can strike, without warning and without mercy. They know that symptoms can mean cancer. How can they live 'normal' lives after this experience? The fear of cancer coming back can become all-consuming, driven by 'normal' aches and pains, twisted into 'evidence' their cancer has come back.

The paralysing fear of recurrence – what can be done?

The truth is that there are no certainties. Yes, doctors may say the cancer is 'gone', Dr Google may quote wonderful figures, but the reality is that there is no absolute certainty. While the (often annoying) phrase 'one can be hit by a bus' is true, the reality is most people, who have not had cancer, do not really consider this as a possibility. They blithely live their lives believing disasters will happen – **to someone else**. They live, in effect, in a form of **communal denial**. But, as someone with cancer knows, disasters can, and do, happen – without warning, without blame and despite efforts to the contrary.

So the person with cancer must find ways to return to that 'blithe certainty' but with a difference, knowing that, for them, the bus has already hit and can hit again. For many patients, the passage of time is enough for this 'return to blithe certainty' to happen. As the weeks and months pass and they remain well, their anxiety lessens, as do their thoughts of cancer. For others, however, like Linda, the fear persists, 'infecting' their thoughts, invading their lives.

The Story of Mary A and Mary B

As we have discussed, not all fear is unhelpful. In fact, some worry is helpful, motivating us to act, prompting us to consider helpful plans. However, for people like Linda, the worry is 'out of control', all-pervasive. For Linda, **the cost of worrying is too high**. It is no longer helpful. The fear that cancer **might come back** is very different from a fear that **cancer might happen** – for patients with cancer that 'bus' has already struck. Yet by continuing to experience the anxiety and fears, despite being 'cured' of cancer, they have not 'got their life back'. Yes, the cancer is gone, but it is still invading every part of their lives, in some cases preventing them from living at all.

Listening to our patients tell of these experiences, we

realised we needed to come up with new strategies for our patients. Existing strategies in CBT (cognitive behaviour therapy), a very useful technique in mainstream mental health, did not translate well to the reality of our patients with cancer. While developing a manual for cancer-related fatigue for our patients at St James's Hospital, Dublin (Collier S, O'Dwyer A M, *How to Manage Persistent Cancer-Related Fatigue, St James's Hospital, Dublin, 2011*), Dr Collier and I developed a series of 'stories', which we discussed with patients gripped by these fears, including the story of 'Mary A and Mary B'.

Mary A, Mary B, Anne A, Anne B

We imagine two patients Mary and Anne (or Liam and John if you prefer), both aged 42, both active people before being diagnosed with cancer, now finished treatment and 'cured'. We know (because this is a story) that Mary's cancer will come back in 10 years' time and she will have to deal with it then, while Anne will die, asleep in her bed, aged 92. Mary and Anne have two very different possible approaches to living their lives post cancer. We have called them A or B.

Mary A worries all the time that her cancer will return. She constantly questions why she got cancer, checks and monitors herself for any sign of illness. She spends much of her time at her GP, or in the hospital, to check that she is well. While she is reassured briefly, her worries quickly return, sometimes overwhelming her with panic attacks. She cannot return to work because of the panic attacks. She avoids family and friends, who inevitably either say 'the wrong thing' and make her fears worse or are irritable with her for constantly seeking reassurance. She cannot book a holiday as she imagines what will happen if she gets ill while abroad and her cancer returns. She avoids any exercise as someone has told her that rest is very important to keep well.

This is how Mary A lives for 10 years. For 10 years she monitors her body, she doesn't eat or sleep well, she avoids any contact with friends or family, she rarely leaves the house. After 10 years her cancer comes back and she starts back into treatment.

Mary B takes a very different approach to her cancer. She says to herself, 'Today I am well. I don't know what will happen tomorrow or next year, but there is no reason why today can't be a good day.' Mary B embraces her life. She goes to all her (booked) medical appointments, but otherwise does not dwell on her cancer returning. She meets her friends and family, goes on holiday, returns to her exercise (slowly, building up her fitness) and returns to work, enjoying the challenges of her work and interactions with her colleagues.

This is how Mary B lives for 10 years. She lives each day as it comes, she sleeps and eats well, living by the saying 'Today I am well.' After 10 years, her cancer comes back and she starts back into treatment.

Anne A and Anne B

Anne A takes the same approach to life as Mary A. She constantly checks her body for signs of cancer recurrence. She neither sleeps nor eats well, avoiding family and friends, unable to return to work, meet colleagues or go on holiday. She is very sad about the 'loss of her old life', becoming sadder every day that passes, as she spends most of her time thinking about cancer.

Anne A lives like this for another fifty years until she dies in her sleep.

Anne B *has the same attitude to her life as Mary B. 'I don't know what will happen tomorrow but there is nothing I can do about that today.' Like Mary B, she socialises with friends and family, returns to a job she enjoyed and sleeps and eats well.*

Anne B lives like this for another fifty years until she dies in her sleep.

Almost invariably, when we asked patients who were often racked by anxiety and distress, which person they would like to be, unsurprisingly, most people choose Anne B – her cancer does not come back and she has a very good quality of life. But when told they cannot be Anne B, they must choose either Mary A, Mary B or Anne A, most people choose Mary B, whose cancer comes back. We always ask why not choose Anne A, who gets to live to be 92? The reply of most of our patients, themselves struggling with the horrific, crippling, paralysing effects of anxiety and therefore understanding its cruel impact, is 'Anne A has no life at all.'

Considering the stories of Mary and Anne is the first step for patients to consider the option of having a life free from cancer worries – an appropriate place for people who have already had the burden of a cancer diagnosis and treatment.

For those with severe anxiety, it will need more than reading, it will require dedicated psychological expertise. For others, simply acknowledging the fact and recognising the patterns can be enough to help them to move forward.

The recurrent 'check-ups'

The sense of support and sharing with others, the regular reassurance and support from staff, the structure and routine, the safety of the hospital environment, ironically these are often sorely, and unexpectedly, missed when treatment ends.

Instead you will now have intermittent 'check-ups' – challenges in themselves. It is very common for people to have a dramatic increase in anxiety in the days (or even weeks) immediately before 'review' or 'check-up' appointments. The days waiting for test results to become available have been described as 'torture' by some people. In these heightened states of anxiety and stress, many of the former unhelpful thinking patterns may become active – *the delay in hearing the results means the results are terrible, the cancer is back* (as opposed to backlogs in the administrative process); the doctor approaching with a sad face or tense look means that *the results are terrible* (as opposed to the doctor having their own issues); your appointment being moved forward means *bad news* as opposed to a cancellation.

As has been the question in almost every example so far in this book – *How helpful are these thought processes for you? How much of your life has been taken away, how many days have been eroded by this worry? Will it make the cancer less likely to be back?*

So, while it is absolutely, understandably, extremely anxiety-provoking to have to go back into the hospital environment where you had your treatment, to be brought face to face again with your cancer, for your sake it is worth looking at strategies that you might use to reduce that anxiety.

- Try to arrange activities that will engage you in the days before tests or review appointments.
- 'Watch out' for unhelpful thinking patterns already discussed and tackle them.
- Ensure you have regularly 'timetabled' mindfulness, relaxation, yoga – whatever works for you.
- If necessary, set aside a 'worry time' each day. Make a note of what your worries are and examine them to see if any are helpful.
- Recognise that, as in the past, whatever comes your way, you can plan strategies once you have proper information.
- In the meantime, focus on today – nothing has changed from last week or last month, other than your forthcoming appointment.

Unhelpful behaviours

Uncertainty is a recurrent theme for people who have had cancer. The 'end of treatment' means stepping away from the 'certainty' of the treatment plan. When faced with uncertainty, a reasonable response is to 'be extra careful', to check, to seek more information and/or seek reassurance. Some of these strategies are, in fact, very unhelpful.

Checking

It is common, even appropriate, to check yourself for any sign of change or illness post cancer treatment. However, as always, it depends on the context and the frequency. If done too frequently, or incorrectly, it can become a problem. For example, feeling for lumps so often that you leave yourself sore, or cause skin changes or swelling will only cause anxiety to rise; or feeling for your pulse rate, which can cause your heart rate to increase, which further increases your anxiety. These behaviours also mean that your thoughts are focused only, or mainly, on your cancer – not on the rest of your life. Ask your doctors about what is appropriate and helpful for you. Some may advise you to check once a month – schedule a day for this, for example the first Monday of every month. Others may advise you not to check at all – to wait until your review appointment.

Hypervigilance

Hypervigilance is similar to checking – constantly 'scanning' your body for anything that seems unusual. People do it because they feel it will alert them early to identify any threat. However, hypervigilance also means that we become aware of normal bodily sensations (that we would otherwise not notice) and we decide that they are 'dangerous', causing us to worry more, leading to more checking – and so the vicious cycle continues. Furthermore, it can stop you from doing things that keep you healthy, such as exercising, and may cause you to have multiple unnecessary tests.

As always, however, a note of caution and balance is needed. If you have had cancer, especially if it has been 'missed' before, you will be very concerned that this may happen again. A good plan is to have a discussion with your (trusted) cancer doctor as to what will likely serve you best.

Information gathering

Following her diagnosis of cancer, Darragh wanted to get as much information as possible about her illness and treatment. She was searching for information that would reduce her uncertainty about surviving cancer. She would listen to stories from her friends about people they knew who had cancer, she read any newspaper or magazine article she could find and she spent many hours on the internet.

However, she found that many of the media stories focused on the negative, with frightening, often contradictory reports. She was unable to 'sieve' through the information for what was true. The more she heard, the less certain she was, the more anxious and frightened she became.

Getting information is a reasonable approach to threat. In this book, we have repeatedly said 'Information is power.' We have qualified that and said **the right information** is power. Seeking information from the wrong sources can lead to a feeling of less, rather than more, control and certainty.

What can you do instead? As with 'hypervigilance', ask your cancer team for the information you want. Use your 'check-up' appointment. Bring a relative with you to help you remember the answers. Ask them to direct you to useful sources of information.

Reassurance-seeking

While you are attending regularly for treatment, you will be able to easily access reassurance from the staff that you meet. Once you 'end' treatment, you lose easy access to that source of reassurance.

Seeking someone's opinion, or reassurance, is a very helpful strategy if:

1. There is a definite answer to the question being asked.
2. The person you have asked is the appropriate person.
3. You believe their answer.

Reassurance-seeking becomes a problem when you can't just seek it once or twice or even three times, but go back time and time again. Problematic, repeated reassurance-seeking only makes you calmer in the short term. Soon (often within 24 hours), you will again doubt the reassurance. You say to yourself *'Maybe I didn't make myself clear; maybe I didn't ask the right question, maybe he mixed up my results; was he really listening? Why didn't she send me for a scan?'*

So, while reassurance-seeking brings benefits **briefly**, ultimately it is short-lived. Furthermore, it can have a very negative impact on our health experience. Some doctors become anxious themselves and may send you for unnecessary tests that can be harmful. Others become so accustomed to interpreting your queries in the context of anxiety that they may miss a new query. Finally, in most cases it is not possible for anyone to give an absolute guarantee that everything is perfect – the so-called 'medical all-clear'.

What can you do?

It is, of course, difficult with a recent cancer diagnosis. Some cancers will need monitoring. Frank conversation with your cancer team, acknowledging your anxiety, is helpful. You may be able to create a 'decision plan' with them. This can detail what symptoms need to be seen immediately, what can wait. You can document what symptoms you have had previously, what the results were, whether this is a new symptom, worse or better, etc. As always, bringing someone with you to these discussions is a good idea.

Other strategies

It is entirely understandable to be worried about your health after cancer. As we have repeatedly said, your 'bus' has already hit. You **know** that bad things can happen – even when you have been healthy and careful. In addition to the practical steps described above, you may want to use some of the strategies below, useful in the management of worry and anxiety.

Worry time

If you find that you seem to be constantly worrying, set aside a specific time to worry each day – usually in the **early** evening (not close to bedtime). Then, every time an anxious thought comes to you, say to yourself that you will focus on that in your 'worry time'. Set aside 30 minutes, in a quiet place, write out in a jotter, and examine, your worries. Do not get up until your 30 minutes are up. If, after a few days, you notice 30 minutes is too long, try reducing your time to 20 minutes. During the rest of the day, any time you find yourself worrying jot the thoughts down in a notebook to deal with later, or simply say to yourself you will note it later.

This practice of setting aside a 'time' to worry:
- allows a sense of control over worries
- shows that you do not need to worry **every minute** of the day
- you can use that time instead to do something that you enjoy, or need to do
- highlights how repetitive worries usually are – while you may seem to have hundreds of worries, you probably have only a few worries that keep repeating.

Thought suppression and avoidance

Most people avoid anything unpleasant – it is an entirely understandable response. Some, seeking to feel as certain as possible, try to push all thoughts of cancer to the back of their mind. This is like pushing a large ball under water in a swimming pool. Yes, you can do it. But it requires enormous constant effort and ultimately bounces back up again – sometimes in a different place. Typically, the harder we try to force a thought out of our mind, the stronger it bounces back. This is true of all thoughts, but especially troubling ones.

Try the following 'experiment'.
Put down this book and for the next 20 seconds you can think about anything you wish, except for one thing. I want you to try as hard as you can **not to think** of a large white bear. Do **not** think about that big white bear, with large white paws and pointed ears. What happened?! For most of us,

simply trying to put something out of our mind makes it take over.

What can you do instead?

Stop trying to force thoughts out of your mind. Notice them, acknowledge them. Then focus instead on an activity or event that you find interesting or enjoyable. Worrying thoughts may pop into your head but the frequency will drop as there is no 'rebound' effect. You will also gain so much more from your day as you devote time to activities you like, rather than spending time and energy trying to keep thoughts at bay.

'When treatment ends' is a misnomer. 'When rehabilitation starts' is a better term. Where you are headed, as your active treatment draws to a close, is the **rehabilitation phase**. Knowing in advance that this phase can bring many challenges is the first step in taking charge of the process, ensuring that it is a move in a positive direction, lessening the disappointment, shame and sense of failure that so many patients feel when they step off the treadmill of treatment and head to rejoin their families and friends. And it is, in truth, another 'stepping stone'. Your rehabilitation phase leads you into another phase – reaching your baseline, and **beyond your baseline**. So 'well done' on getting through treatment. Now the focus is on rehabilitating yourself, heading towards a more 'normal' existence, reclaiming your life after cancer.

12

After Cancer – Reclaiming Your Life: Choices, Physical Health and Work

This chapter focuses on the time when acute treatment and side-effects have abated. It focuses on the time **after** the period of 'rehabilitation' after treatment ends, already described, usually at least six months after the end of cancer treatment, probably closer to a year or more. You will have been through the diagnosis, finished treatment and (possibly) experienced some of the challenges discussed earlier, such as distress, anxiety, depression, cancer-related fatigue, body-image problems. Now you are looking at your life, thinking – *where to from here?*

Some of our patients have told us that the whole experience of going through cancer has led them to re-assess their lives. They want to review their priorities, preciously guard their time, live every moment. Deciding when, and how, to do this can be very difficult.

Cancer and the freedom to make choices

It is extremely difficult to consider a cancer diagnosis in anything other than a negative light. Yet many people, once they have recovered from their diagnosis and treatment, review their lives. They make new judgements. They use the experience of cancer described in earlier chapters – the sense of their lives being 'tossed up in the air and waiting for the pieces to land' – to decide where they now want those pieces to land. And it is not always in the same place they were before cancer. Toxic relationships, toxic friends, toxic jobs – all are examined with a cold and clinical eye in the context of the hard facts of knowing, of experiencing the fact that life is short and we do not know what is around the corner. This is the knowledge that patients who have had cancer have, which the average person on the street does not have. They believe, they know, that life is fragile. The rest of us, who have not had that experience, close our eyes and hope and pretend it will not happen to us. And, as a result, we may miss opportunities. There is an 'official' name for this process – 'post-traumatic growth'. Not everyone who has had cancer is willing to consider this. Some regard it as a further assault to suggest that their experience could be viewed in anything other than a negative light. Others find it helpful, now that they have finished treatment, to view it as a chance to start with a new focus. Would one volunteer to have cancer to experience this? I do not think so. But, having had cancer and, again, grasping back any control that this can give you, re-examining your life and your goals can be a very useful path forward. Not everyone wants to do this. But for those that do, below are some of the ways you might consider.

Liam was a very successful businessman, husband, father of three children under 12, who had recently finished his cancer treatment.

He had always felt he was a very good 'provider' for his family – something that he hugely valued. However, he had a long commute to work every day. He left his house every morning at 6 o'clock and returned at 7 o'clock in the evening. While his work was very rewarding, it was also extremely stressful. He was responsible for a significant part of the governance of the company and he had begun to realise that this responsibility rarely left his mind. Furthermore, one of his business partners was truly toxic, very difficult to manage. He realised that, every time he met them, he left feeling stressed and on edge. All of this he brought home with him, tired and exhausted, late in the evening.

Part of his recovery from cancer had meant him spending long periods at home, slowly rehabilitating. For the first time in years, he had been able to spend time with his children during the day, listening to what had happened at school, seeing their homework, their arts and crafts, and refereeing their squabbles. He got to watch them training in the evenings and support their teams. He also had time to reflect on the points above. He knew he had some difficult decisions to make. There would be significant financial implications if there were to be any changes in his role.

Working with the psycho-oncology service, Liam decided to re-evaluate his life before cancer. Using the strategies described below, he recharted his priorities, made a plan to approach his work, and worked with his wife to agree areas they would prioritise together.

Rechart your life

Consider the activities that you do

Make a list of **how you spend your time at present**. Examples may include: work, housework, family, friends, sleep (including naps), reading, hobbies, physical activity, travel, religion. You will have your own list.

Give each of these a percentage (roughly) and then convert this into what we call a pie chart – a round diagram – giving each activity a section. This makes it easier to see how much of your life is spent doing these things. You may be surprised at the results!

Liam wrote out his list of activities, converted them to pie charts and examined how he spent his time before cancer, immediately after cancer, and then as he improved. He then drew out how he would like to spend them now – and was very surprised by the differences. He spoke at length to his wife, several close friends and his management team at work. Ultimately, he made very significant changes to his 'work' and 'non-work' times.

Reclaiming your life 'beyond your baseline' – a practical approach

Life can be rewarding, rich and meaningful. However, after cancer many people's routine has become hugely reduced, and many of their usual activities (and people) avoided. Bearing in mind what people have said about reclaiming their lives 'for the better' after cancer, consider what your ideal life would be – what activities would you want to add, subtract, increase? What activities have you never done before, but always intended to do? Now is the time! So that it is not simply about reaching your baseline. If you wish, you can **go beyond your baseline, reclaim your life in a new way**. But first there will be structures and challenges to consider.

Physical activity

Walking

Physical activity, using our muscles, strengthening our bones, is so important to keep us well, especially as we age, and particularly after a major illness like cancer. And what about if we can 'achieve' multiple targets together. What about if we can exercise, *and* immerse ourselves in nature *and* socialise – we will have achieved several targets of wellbeing.

Bring it into your regular routine – so that it will become **automatic**. Below are some suggestions. You can choose what will suit you best.

- Walk to the shops, always. Only consider other options if you absolutely must.
- Walk to meet friends, walk with friends. Set up a walking group that meets twice a week.
- Invest in good outdoor gear so that you don't look at the weather when deciding about a walk (essential in Ireland).

- Have a dog – they will insist on a walk every day (sometimes two) – and having a pet has been associated with a richer longer life. (They also bring significant responsibilities, so make this decision carefully.)

Yoga, pilates and other forms of muscle toning, stretching and building

These activities, while they are a form of exercise, provide very different activities from 'going for a walk'. They target specific muscle groups and 'core strength' (pilates), or focus on stretching, muscle tone and promoting release from tension and awareness of one's body (yoga). They can also provide a social context if you join a weekly class. Invest in some weights – an essential item to help reduce muscle and bone loss as we age.

Your physiotherapist will be a good source of advice about how this may, or may not, be helpful for you.

Combine social and physical rehabilitation

Joining a walking group or even a dance class (suggested by one adventurous patient) allows you to combine physical and social rehabilitation.

Healthy eating

Good nutrition has an important role to play during your physical recovery from cancer. In the early stages of your treatment you may find it very difficult to eat anything at all. The effects of surgery, chemotherapy and other treatments on appetite, nausea and swallowing, can all combine to make eating a significant challenge. Furthermore, the conflicting advice you may receive about what you may or may not eat, particularly if you have had intensive chemotherapy and are afraid of infection, may make it difficult for you to resume normal eating. As you move away from your cancer treatment phase, establishing a healthy eating pattern is an important part of your recovery process.

Like almost every other behaviour post cancer, you may have to approach this as a structured exercise. Make a plan for this, gradually increasing the amount and variety of food you take. Ask your nutrition expert on your team for advice if necessary. I have included some general tips for healthy eating below. As you recover from cancer, it may seem daunting to look down this list as even more 'tasks' for you to do. Consider enlisting the help of a friend to do some of the shopping, or even the food preparation, for you.

Calculate what is a healthy weight range for you – and stay within that range

There are several websites that will help you to calculate a healthy weight. These generally will include your height as well as your weight to give you a figure that is called your BMI (Body Mass Index) – your weight in kg over your height in metre squared. Using your height as well as your weight helps to ensure the final figure is more representative of your physique. Please take care when researching this on the internet and use a reputable website, as there are many websites that provide harmful misinformation about weight and diet.

Suggestions for healthy eating

- Eat at regular, spaced intervals in the day and include a high-fibre food with each meal (eg wholegrain cereal).
- Eat five or more fruit or vegetables a day. Eating a variety of colours of fruit and vegetables will help make sure that you get a wide range of vitamins and minerals. You should not need extra supplements if you are eating well. Discuss with your nutritionist if you are unsure.
- Choose fresh, rather than processed, foods.
- Eat at least two portions of fish a week, including at least one portion of oily fish.
- Choose a wide variety of food, including poultry and a maximum of 500 g of cooked red lean meat (beef, lamb, pork) per week.
- Avoid 'fast foods' and sugary drinks and keep alcohol and salt to a minimum.

If, despite trying these, you find you are still losing weight, or, if you find it impossible to follow this plan, please speak to your cancer team nutritionist for advice.

Fun

Having struggled through cancer, diagnosis and treatment, it can be very difficult to even say the word 'fun', let alone consider bringing it into your life. But 'fun' is a key part of wellbeing. Everyone's definition of what 'fun' is varies. I have had patients who have taken up a new language; gone to ballroom dancing classes; started a painting course; joined a choir. The list is endless. Doing something new, creative, spontaneous, is good for your brain and your wellbeing. And remember the activities pie chart at the beginning of the chapter. No time for fun? Maybe some of the other pie pieces need to be made smaller.

Other activities to consider

Other important aspects of wellbeing to consider include promoting your night-time sleep; setting aside time when you get to 'check' on yourself, reflect on what is happening for you (without getting hijacked by rumination); simple tasks where you develop your concentration (crosswords, word games, number games – whatever you enjoy). And you can be strategic – plan something that incorporates many areas. When I started a wellbeing project for junior doctors at SJH, Dublin, I set up a choir that met every week, at lunchtime. As a group, it gave us a novel creative experience (more novel for some than others), an opportunity to socialise, gain some 'down-time' from work, get physical exercise, focus on a task and engage with a wider audience, experiencing the pleasure of bringing pleasure to others by singing for patients and staff. Planning your tasks strategically can allow you to do several things together – if that is what you would like.

Returning to work after cancer

Returning to work after cancer is a hugely important part of reclaiming their lives for many people. People's relationships with their work vary enormously. For some, work is a drudge that must be endured; for others, it is a stimulating rewarding environment that provides structure (psychological and social), as well as financial rewards. For most, the reality lies somewhere between those two extremes. Most will, however, need to return to work after cancer. This can pose many challenges.

Sean, a young man, an engineer in a large company, was diagnosed with cancer three months after his wedding. He and his wife were devastated. He got through his diagnosis and treatment, keeping a 'brave face' throughout. He was determined to get back to work as soon as his treatment finished.

He was devastated when, at the end of treatment, he found himself completely exhausted. Barely able to leave the house, he recognised he could not manage the two-hour commute to work, working nine hours a day on site. He felt guilty, 'useless' and demoralised. He was extremely stressed and anxious about his job. He had told HR that he would be back as soon as his treatment was over. Now, thinking of returning to work made him feel he was standing at the edge of a large chasm he would never be able to cross. He felt a failure, just married and already he could not support his family. Overwhelmed, he could not see a way forward.

Helping Sean with his return to work brings together much of what we have already discussed. The first step was listening to his story and allowing him to speak. A diligent worker all his life, whose rules for living included that one worked hard and didn't complain, he found it very difficult to 'admit' that he was struggling. He had been too ashamed to even voice these fears to anyone. Letting him know that this happened often for people after cancer, that it was an entirely reasonable and a valid position was the first step. Being clear that going back to work was not an immediate option, took the pressure off, gave him the 'breathing space' to properly plan how he might return. An honest, hard-working, conscientious person, being told that, not only was it 'okay' not to go back to work just yet, but that the best, most appropriate way to ensure that he could return to work was to plan for it, freed him from the unhelpful daily guilty thoughts and feelings and allowed him to plan a graded return to work.

Review of the role of work in Sean's life

As has already been said, many people use their experience with cancer to review their lives. Sometimes this includes reviewing the role of work. You may decide you want to return exactly as before; or work fewer hours; or work some hours from home; or move to a different department, or a different firm. Now is a good time to make this review because, as with many situations post cancer, whatever you eventually do, you will manage best if you **review** and **plan** your strategies.

Sean wanted to continue with his work. He enjoyed it, he found it rewarding. It brought structure to his life and he was financially dependent on it. However, he did not feel physically able to return to a full-time role immediately. Furthermore, even before cancer, he had been frustrated by the long hours spent commuting daily. Having had cancer, he was determined to review this and he was very focused now on 'making the most' of every part of his life.

169

Setting realistic achievable goals

The task of returning to work is, in effect, an integration of all the previous tasks we have discussed in reclaiming your life. It incorporates physical, social and emotional tasks. If, like Sean, you have had extensive treatment after cancer, much like returning to physical activity, it is unlikely that, at a set point after your treatment ends, you can, on that day, leave the house and step straight back into full-time work. Everyone recovers at different rates; everyone's cancer, and treatment, is different. It is better to plan an achievable target, rather than plan a target that is overwhelming, that you simply cannot achieve.

Make a plan. Enlist the help of family and friends. Discuss with your cancer, or psycho-oncology team if necessary.

Sean's plan

Sean wanted to return to work. But he agreed that rather than a general goal – 'I will go back to work', he decided on **specific** goals that described exactly what he wanted (and what he felt he was able to do). His ideal was to return to working three days in the office and two days from home. He planned to gradually return to this level of activity – initially working one day per week in the office, moving up to two days after two weeks, etc, planning to review this strategy after four weeks to adapt it if necessary.

Having made his plan, Sean then needed to check if it was realistic. He spoke informally to a senior colleague whom he trusted, to identify if this working pattern might be possible within the firm. He then arranged to meet his Human Resources officer to check that they would agree to his return plan. He spoke to his wife, who was very supportive, and was relieved to hear and understand the worries that he had about returning to work.

Other strategies in Sean's plan

Sean also needed to prepare for the inevitable interpersonal challenges of returning to work, planning strategies for social interactions (discussed in the next chapter). Sean added his own work-related experiences to the list, ranging from being identified as *'the person with cancer'* at all events (something he did not want) to complete lack of acknowledgement of the fact that he had been ill at all (*'Welcome back. We have been run off our feet while you were gone'*). For the first, he met his manager for a private meeting and asked that he not be introduced/identified as the person with cancer. For the second, he prepared a response that thanked the person for the welcome back, noting that he himself had been pretty much run off his feet while away, but that he was glad to be returning to help with the work flow in his job now.

In addition to managing these social encounters, Sean also looked carefully at his list for what he wanted in his life now, highlighting activities outside work that he wanted to continue (football, photography) and social time with his wife and friends.

Others may need to consider how they will manage changes in their physical appearance or physical abilities.

You will need to adapt these goals and interventions to suit yourself. The most important first step is acknowledging that it may be difficult, and sitting down to set out a plan of action, engaging the help of your key personal supports. This does not come naturally to most people who have lived lives before cancer without needing to do this. Sean had found his cancer experience a difficult one and initially struggled with yet another task. Ultimately, he saw this as what he termed 'a wake-up call' to ensure that he now lived his life as he wanted, on his terms.

'Reclaiming' your life includes many of the activities above. It also, inevitably, involves interacting with others. The next chapter looks at examples where these interactions can be challenging, and makes suggestions for managing these in reclaiming your life after cancer.

13

After Cancer – Reclaiming Your Life: Managing Social Situations

Managing social situations – difficult encounters, difficult situations

It may seem odd to include 'people' as an obstacle to reclaiming your life – and to devote an entire chapter to the topic. People, of course, are often key in helping you to 'survive' your cancer journey and to reclaim your life afterwards.

However, many people who have, or have had, cancer find managing social situations and meeting 'other people' stressful – for all stages on their road to recovery. How stressful it is will, as always, depend on the individual – 'you', and your 'usual' way of managing people. Some people are very extrovert and share information easily and readily with everyone. Others are extremely private, keep themselves 'to themselves' and share information only when necessary. And then there are many people somewhere in between.

Cancer – a 'public' diagnosis
The difficulty is that cancer is, so often, a very public diagnosis. Particularly if you live in a small community, word somehow

'gets out'. People may discuss it, approach you to 'sympathise'. These may be people whom you rarely meet otherwise. Many people with cancer find this intrusive and upsetting. They say that they themselves are only getting 'used' to their diagnosis. They are not ready to share and discuss it with others.

Later, some of the longer-term side-effects of treatment mean that even total strangers may assume or guess that you have cancer. This is particularly the case for those who have lost hair due to chemotherapy. Patients have described them-selves as feeling 'vulnerable' and 'helpless'. They describe a sense of rage when total strangers gaze at them sympathet-ically or, 'even worse', comment on their appearance.

Facing the challenge of meeting people

Even when people are getting better, they describe how every trip out of their home makes them feel vulnerable to an 'assault' by well-meaning neighbours. One lady described how she would wait in her home, watching out of the window until a particular neighbour had passed, before she could leave for a walk, as she could not bear to talk to them. Others describe apparently well-meaning but distressing interactions.

Patients always have specific examples of what they experi-enced in social situations that caused them distress. One lady described a neighbour who just crossed the road, averted their gaze and didn't acknowledge her at all. She felt as if she had a contagious disease. It made her angry and distressed. Having endured all she had endured, now she felt she was being treated as an outcast. Another described having total strangers approach her because she had lost all her hair and start loud conversations with her on public transport, asking if she had cancer and how she was managing. She said the only other time she had endured such intrusion was when she was pregnant, when total strangers would ask her about it or even put their hand on her tummy to feel it. Another patient described a neighbour who intruded constantly – in an unhelpful way. She described how they would approach her, compose their face into a sad appearance and ask, mournfully, how she was, nodding sadly throughout.

You may find these stories difficult to believe. In truth, it has been genuinely puzzling to me to consider why people would say these things. I have often been sitting with a patient in the clinic, sometimes having spent weeks working with them to build up their confidence, to then hear them recounting these stories. Even after decades in clinical practice, I still sit there thinking, 'How on earth can the person have thought it was reasonable to say those things?'

But psychological work in general, and this book in particular, is about finding ways to analyse these situations and find practical solutions – objectively and empathically. There is always a way.

Why is this happening?

I always say that people with cancer have enough on their mind without having to worry about everyone else (other than close family and friends). However, sometimes one must, briefly, consider the other person's viewpoint, if only to help you to manage the situation for yourself.

The reality is that most people do not have a clue what to say to people with cancer. The word 'cancer' terrifies them. It makes them consider their own mortality, the concept that *they* might get cancer. It brings cancer into their lives, even in the most remote of ways. And that is something most people don't want to consider unless they absolutely must. So most people are both anxious and ill-informed – a dangerous place to be if one is about to speak. Let us assume that they (mostly) mean well but are anxious and, out of their depth, they often blurt out statements that really are very unhelpful.

Why is it important to consider this? Well, one of the things that cancer patients report is a huge sense of injustice and anger that someone could possibly treat them so insensitively after what they have been through. Understanding that it is (hopefully) due to anxiety and ignorance can help to distance you from that rage and sense of injustice, allowing you to think more clearly and put your strategy into place.

Why does it matter?

It matters for very many reasons. Firstly, all these interactions are combining to make life for you, the person with cancer, even more difficult and distressing. You have enough to manage without adding this to your list.

Secondly, it may seriously hamper your recovery. Part of recovering from the difficult treatments of cancer is a slow rehabilitation back into normal life. This requires physical, psychological and social rehabilitation. At its most basic, some people are unable to fully engage in any proper physical programme because they just do not want to leave their home. One lady would wait for her husband to come home so he could drive her a long way across Dublin to a park where she would be unlikely to meet anyone she knew. And even then, she could not fully relax and enjoy her time in nature and walking because she was constantly scanning the environment for someone she might know. Furthermore, it affected her ability to reclaim her life psychologically and socially as she just could not manage to meet people.

So these reactions have a profound, often unrecognised, impact across many areas of people's recovery.

Managing social situations – what can be done?

As with everything, there are solutions – ways of managing things that can help you.

Firstly, as with many situations in life, you will need to examine exactly what is happening and how it is affecting you. Then devise a plan, rehearse it (yes rehearse it – it will not come easily to you). Then put it into practice.

As I have said earlier, patients with cancer lose a huge amount of control in their lives. You go from being independent, self-sufficient individuals, to being ill and frail patients, feeling you have little control over many of the actions that you previously, naturally, have taken for granted – what you eat, what you can do physically, how you spend your day. Some of what is happening in the conversations above reflects that lack of control, not because these are situations you would have previously experienced, but because these new situations require control to manage them.

So you will need to take control of the conversations, deflect and direct them as you wish. There is a 'scale' of severity for doing this that you can choose from. I smile as I write this because many patients, even in the midst of their own trauma, are 'shocked' by some of my suggestions. Despite having endured so much themselves, they would not dream of choosing from the more severe end of the spectrum. But you do get to choose.

Identify the unhelpful 'themes' in what people say and develop specific replies/ways of managing them

If you look at the examples given already, you will see that people have a 'set' number of responses (generally) in response to meeting someone with cancer. Please do note that I am not suggesting that people are malevolent, or mean ill. Generally, as has already been said, they are simply both anxious and ill-informed. The resulting interactions include the following themes (all based on patient reports):

- Excessively intrusive – 'Is the cancer completely gone?' 'When is your next scan?' 'Do you still have the bowel bag?'
- Too much information about other people's cancer experience – 'My cousin got the "all-clear" after cancer and he was dead two months later'; 'My friend had chemotherapy and her brain was never right afterwards.'
- Public displays of emotion – 'How are you at all, you poor creature? It makes me want to cry myself.'
- Unscientific, unhelpful, conflicting advice –'You need to go to rest', 'You shouldn't rest', 'You should talk about it', 'You shouldn't talk about it', 'You should eat plenty of red meat', 'You shouldn't eat any meat', 'You should

drink pomegranate juice from Chile', 'You should only eat green fruit'.

- Comments about your appearance – 'You look great', 'You look thin', 'What happened to your lovely hair?'
- Determinedly optimistic – 'Well, that's great it's all over now, there's a lot of work to be done for the community party in September.'

When you read down this list, you wonder how patients with cancer venture out at all! Yet you will, and you must. But having a **plan in place** to manage each of these scenarios is very helpful. And you may even use it in a wider context, handling difficult scenarios well removed from cancer as you move into wider settings.

Choose whom you meet and when

It is very easy to become socially isolated after cancer – feeling like no one else can understand or care. Yet you will have had friends (and family) who will have supported you throughout. Meeting friends and returning to your social life is part of the process of recovering from cancer – a step in reclaiming your life. Reading the examples above, one can see why some people stay at home, avoiding social interactions. These can be particularly hard when it is the first time you have seen the person (or group) for some time.

Use the 'steps of the stairs' approach described for physical rehabilitation, for your social interactions. Choose your 'trusted' people for your initial outings. This will slowly give you confidence for other outings. And you may be surprised to find how many have also had experience of cancer. Perhaps then move on to meet others with your 'trusted' friends by your side to help you navigate the next stage.

By choosing carefully whom you meet initially, you are less likely to have to endure the unhelpful comments listed above. But, of course, there will still be chance encounters for which you will need to be ready.

Focus on the other person

The reality is that many people you meet are themselves struggling to know what to say – should they mention cancer? Should they say nothing? Should they just cross the street to avoid the meeting? While you are the person with cancer, and therefore have enough to do in managing your own distress, it is useful to be aware that other people may also be struggling, as this may free you from some of the beliefs you have about them. Remind yourself about the 'myths' about cancer. People who repeat them to you may mean well, but they can be confusing and unhelpful.

Have specific sentences planned to redirect the conversation

Most patients who fear social interaction describe how they feel 'powerless' in the conversation, dreading the comments about cancer, frozen, waiting for them to be said, and then unable to think of a reply.

So, you will need to plan specific sentences. This is the point where I lose most patients initially. They just cannot imagine having to plan a conversation. But that is the reality after cancer (and, indeed, for other situations in life too, for example 'returning to work'). Regard it as being like your physical rehabilitation programme. You may decide to give some information and then redirect or divert the conversation (to a theme they are likely to be interested in).

The list below offers options:

- Redirect to their family – 'I am great, thank you. How is your son getting on in his new job?'
- Redirect to the other person – 'I haven't decided yet about going back to work. How about you? Are you still working?' Or: 'I am fine, thank you. I love that dress you are wearing. Where did you get it?'
- Redirect to recent news – 'Yes, I am still tired but that is improving. Were you watching the football/soccer/hurling/golf at the weekend? Wasn't the news terrible?'
- For the 'strangers' on public transport who ask if you have cancer, you have many options. You can reply 'Why do you ask?', 'Have you had cancer?' (!) or, more benignly, 'I am well, thank you – how are you?' It is the turning of the conversation back on to the other person that is important. It helps to take the focus away from you.

These are what I call the 'polite' options. But sometimes, despite these gentle hints, people plough right on, doggedly bringing the conversation back to your cancer. As always, there is a range of responses available to you:

- Acknowledge they are talking about your illness and you do not want it. 'I am fed up talking about my cancer – what's happening with Mary and her new job?' or 'I'd rather not talk about illness right now, let's focus on something else instead.'

If people are still persistent, and particularly for those who have informed you of their cousin who 'dropped dead of cancer' after their all-clear (for whom I, as a cancer therapist, feel a particular malevolence when hearing a distraught cancer patient recount the distressing experience), you can either go on a direct offensive:

- Do you think that is a helpful thing for me to hear when I am just recovering from cancer myself?

Or, upping the ante a step further, say, mirroring the same long face and doleful air:

- You know, you are looking very peaky yourself. Have you been for a check-up recently? That is exactly how I looked before I got my diagnosis.

Now to be clear, I normally lose all my patients when I get to the last two options. They are usually absolutely shocked at the suggestions and look at me with a slightly perturbed air. Despite often themselves having borne very similar statements (admittedly likely to have come from anxiety rather than ill-will), they just will not consider doing it themselves. And that is fine. Nonetheless, it almost invariably elicits a smile, and does demonstrate, and give back to you, very clearly, the options of **power and control** that you can have if you choose to use it.

Practice

Patients also usually dig their heels in (metaphorically) at this suggestion. They think it is ridiculous. But this is a new scenario for you. Practice will hugely help your ability to manage this situation. Try it and see – with your therapist or a family member. And swap roles after a few goes – you be the concerned friend and they be the person recovering from cancer. Reflect on how that feels.

Managing social situations – remembering the positives

It is important to remember that, of course, there are often many positive examples of the support, sustenance and well-being that interacting with others – particularly families and friends – can bring.

Leah had not had surgery for her cancer. She had no visible scars. But she had been left feeling utterly physically exhausted by her treatment. A single lady in her early 30s, her physical fitness had been a central part of her life. She was a keen member of her local athletic and running and walking clubs, spending almost all her leisure time in physical activity with her local groups.

Following her cancer treatment, she felt utterly demoralised. She could barely make it up the stairs. How could she possibly ever face her friends? They would want nothing to do with her – she would only slow them all down. She refused all phone calls, locked her door and hid in her house, becoming more and more miserable.

Luckily for Leah, her friends were persistent. They continued to call to the door, leaving messages, cards, even food. Eventually she allowed them to come in and they began to talk. One morning, they finally got her to agree to leave the house and walk to the end of her housing estate with them. She stepped out into a beautiful spring day, saw for the first time in many months the daffodils in clumps around the neighbourhood trees, took a deep breath of fresh air and began to walk towards the end of the estate. To her surprise, she found she could easily keep up with her athletic friends. 'I am not as bad as I thought I was,' she thought to herself. Then she saw Mrs O Brien, her neighbour from the end house, a lady in her late eighties who walked slowly with a cane, overtake them with ease on the far side of the street. And Leah stopped and understood. Her kind, wonderful, supportive friends cared so much for her that, without saying a word, they had slowed their speed right down to the slow halting steps she was taking. And in that moment, in the early sunshine of a promising day she knew that she would get better, that what she needed was faith in herself and faith in her friends.

Leah's story is a lovely example of how encounters with friends provide many things at once – friendship, warmth, sharing, boosting, helping with physical exercise, encounters with nature and being part of a 'team' – the knowledge that you are not alone. Most people **want** to help. They often just do not know how best to do this, how to 'handle' cancer themselves. So you may have to help them out – help them to help you. You may be at the stage in your cancer where you are just too exhausted to do this – elect someone you love and trust to take the lead in this if so. Have them read the chapter for family and friends, and allow them to take the lead in helping you.

Other challenges to reclaiming your life

Waiting for the 'perfect moment'

Perhaps one of the biggest obstacles to reclaiming your life is 'waiting for the perfect moment'; waiting for something to happen first – perhaps something physical (for example, waiting for your hair to grow back the way it was before), or waiting to feel fit again, or waiting for some family event. But while you are waiting, life and time are continuing to tick by. And, the longer you wait, the more difficult it becomes to reclaim your life.

Joanna was a 28-year-old architect who had finished cancer treatment, but remained on steroids after a bone-marrow transplant. These had caused her weight to increase, her muscles to waste and her hair (previously her 'pride and joy') to become thin. She desperately wanted to return to work, but she did not want to go back until she had 'returned to normal', and 'looked right'. She decided to wait until things were better, she was off steroids, her weight had stabilised and her hair was back to normal.

Every time her steroids were reduced, they had to be increased again. By the time she attended for her psycho-oncology appointment, she had finished treatment two years earlier, her cancer was 'cured', but she still had not gone back to work.

Because she was at home, on her own, full time, she became more and more upset, focused on her cancer and her treatment. Going back to work seemed more, not less, difficult. The longer it went on, the more difficult it seemed to become.

No one in her family wanted to challenge her. Everyone felt she had had a difficult time. Why would they want to upset her more by 'forcing her' to go out and meet people?

This is a difficult situation. But when Joanna sat down and looked at her life, she realised that what she wanted was to be back at work at a job she loved, with company she enjoyed. She wanted to go out, meet friends, have fun. She had been 'waiting for the perfect moment' for more than two years. And during that time, she had lost two years of her life, and been increasingly miserable.

Joanna had a choice. She could continue to wait for 'the perfect moment', potentially losing another two years of her life or she could go back now, in a phased way, less than perfectly, but grab that chance now.

Joanna did not spend too much time looking at the alternatives. She did not want to spend another two years waiting for the perfect moment. She chose now, this moment, imperfect as it was, to begin to reclaim her life.

When the loss of something 'vital' causes us to give up on everything

We have already heard, in earlier chapters, about the painful, often overwhelming, effects of cancer and its treatment. Surviving cancer comes at a cost. Some of the costs, while difficult, are temporary and can be overcome (fatigue, depression, physical changes) and hopefully this book will have helped you in addressing these. Some, however, may be permanent. In our work with patients with cancer, **infertility** has been the most devastating issue for many of our patients.

We have already discussed infertility and its implications. We are revisiting this here in the context of how **losing something 'vital'** like fertility **can cause you to give up on everything else**.

Carol was 26 when she discovered she had cancer. Recently married, she had been planning to have children – a key aspiration throughout her life. While she was relieved to learn her cancer treatment had been successful, she was absolutely devastated by the news that she was now infertile.

Carol could not see a way forward for herself. All her friends were having babies. She found it difficult to go to shopping centres or her GP – babies and children seemed to be everywhere. She could not speak to her husband, feeling he could not possibly love her now that she couldn't have children. Going back to work was impossible – she could not bear the endless discussion of babies and children. Increasingly isolated and alone, Carol found it difficult to go on.

As has been the case in many of the cancer stories we have heard, this is a truly heart-breaking and difficult story. Helping Carol to reclaim her life, despite being 'clear' of cancer, is difficult. During conversations with Carol at her psycho-oncology appointments, her replies to me during discussions about reclaiming her life would include 'Haven't I been through enough?' or 'Can you help me to have children? No? Then there is nothing you can do.'

Carol's family and friends, were, understandably, reluctant to challenge her about this. Yet standing by, watching Carol become increasingly isolated, unable to reclaim any of her life in the face of this loss, is not, in truth, a 'kind' option.

This concept, deciding how to reclaim most of something rather than discarding everything was addressed by psychologist Robert Leahy, author of *The Worry Cure*. Leahy notes that the most helpful thing to do when something goes wrong or missing in life is to ask what we *can still do*. He suggests that rather than focus on what has gone wrong, to the detriment of everything else, we turn to our life's 'menu' and look at what we can do.

Leahy was not talking about cancer when developing these ideas. Yet, if you find that struggling with loss in one area means that **every other area in your life is neglected**, and that this has lasted for many months, it may help to consider the 'menu' solution.

In Carol's case, she found the courage to look at what she could do. She engaged with her husband, kind and concerned, full of love for her, but unsure how to support her. She focused on how much she had enjoyed her work. She decided to return to those areas, the areas she still had, even though there were some areas she had to give up on – for now. It was a very difficult step for her to take, but was the first step in an important journey for her.

'Reclaiming' life after cancer can pose many challenges – managing social situations, waiting for the 'right moment', facing inconsolable loss. However, working in psycho-oncology with people who have had a long struggle with a cancer diagnosis and treatment, now 'cured' of cancer, but still 'trapped', unable to reclaim their lives, has pushed us to work with them to find ways to intervene – even when, at times, intervening can seem hard. We hope that in providing examples, worked on with our patients, you will be able to adapt them so that you, too, perhaps helped by family and friends, can reclaim your lives.

Section V

YOUR CANCER AND OTHERS

14

Families and Friends

It is truly devastating, in truth it is impossible to describe, the feeling that hits us when someone we love and hold dear is diagnosed with any illness, particularly cancer, the subject of this book. So often I have heard family members say, 'If only it were me, I would do anything to take it away from them.' This is particularly true for parents of young children/ teenagers or young adults. Most relatives describe the unbearable pain of watching someone they love suffering, and the feelings of powerlessness that it causes. They feel they are 'standing by' 'just watching'.

Ironically, patients themselves often acknowledge this, saying that they are so preoccupied by their cancer and its treatment they cannot often 'take it all in'. Yet they are conscious that their relatives, fully aware and watching them suffer, are sometimes suffering more.

Families and friends of someone with cancer almost always want 'to do something'. But often they don't know what to do, don't understand how best to help. Throughout this book you will have read that there is a range of possible interventions to help patients with cancer. Families and friends can be part of that response. Some suggestions are embedded in the chapters themselves. Below are some other suggestions that I hope may be helpful.

Sit there – don't 'just do something'

A feeling of powerlessness in the face of someone's suffering almost always makes one want to 'do something' – to help. Sometimes, it is, understandably, to help the person distract themselves from the suffering and distress they are witnessing. But for the person in pain and distress, sometimes all they want is for someone they care about to listen; for that person to try to understand what is happening to them, to hear what it is like for them to be experiencing the pain, the fear, the terror, the uncertainty. They do not want to be offered solutions – or platitudes. Too often, they know there may not be any. They just want someone to say, 'I hear you.' Or to say nothing at all, but just sit with them while they endure their suffering and distress. To show you are listening and are with them. This may mean putting the phone/tablet/newspaper/ TV away. Just to sit with them.

Please be aware this is very different from saying, 'I know' or 'I understand'. Sadly, or fortunately, depending on your perspective, one cannot fully know or understand what it is like for the person sitting in front of you, viewing their life and the full implications of their cancer diagnosis – and the person with cancer knows that. Simply hearing them, validating their experience, is what is important.

Tolerate distress – and irritation

It is extremely difficult to sit with someone who is consumed by distress. Most people, understandably, want to avoid it. Yet often that is what the person in distress needs. They need to know that they and their seemingly intolerable situation are tolerable to the person they love the most. And that you can sit with them and not be afraid or overwhelmed.

Similarly, the person in distress may lash out, unreasonably, at the person to whom they are closest, whom they most need; the reaction driven by pain, distress or even an overwhelming sense of injustice that this has happened to them. Again, sit with them (though there are limits to this).

Educate yourself about the cancer and its treatment
A recurring message in this book is 'information is power' – 'forewarned is forearmed'. You will be best able to help your loved one by knowing, as best you can, what they will face. But please note:

- Ensure you get your information from a reliable source. Telling your relative with cancer about a story you have just seen on the internet saying that juicing tea-grass on the slopes of the Andes is the latest treatment for cancer is not likely to be helpful.
- The information needed is not so much about facts and figures, prognosis and mortality, but how you can be best placed to help them (for example understanding how they may feel when treatment ends, or the challenges in reclaiming their lives)
- Keep information to yourself until asked. Information is not for you to constantly update your relative on facts and figures. It is for you, to help you to anticipate their needs and help their recovery.

- If possible, and if they agree, attend their out-patient visits with them, make notes and help them process it later. Distress, fear, pain, medication, sleeplessness can all combine to make it difficult, if not impossible, for the person with cancer to take in all the information they are given. It can be a huge help for them to check with you. But be mindful of the preceding point – wait to be asked, give the information gently. Sometimes, people haven't heard all the information because they are not yet ready to hear it all.

Be practical

I cannot overstate the importance of this point. It can often seem just too mundane, too ordinary to count as helping someone with cancer. But these are the tasks that often are impossible for someone with cancer – and the tasks that most distress them when they cannot do them – the ordinary, mundane household and family tasks of daily life.

Even when a person has cancer, the family still has to be fed, children collected from school, homework checked, shopping done, dogs walked, bins left out – or whatever the practical tasks of everyday life that this person has. These everyday tasks cannot be done by the person with cancer, and often cannot be done or even considered by their closest relative, themselves often overwhelmed by distress. Identify a core group of people to help. Most true friends are desperate to help. Many are relieved to be given something practical to do. Nominate a person to be in charge of the group, and draw up a rota for the necessary tasks. Most people will be happy to do a task once a week, and, if there are enough people on the rota, that will take care of every day using the list of tasks above – school runs; evening meals; school lunches; dog-walking. This rota should include someone who will liaise with the hospital staff, to identify what might be needed after discharge. This might include getting access to a wheelchair or changing the layout of the home.

You will need to work out how to do this without intruding on the person with cancer. For example, sometimes they will just not feel able to meet and thank the person delivering the help. Enlisting practical people, perhaps even explaining these facts to them, may be hugely helpful. Finding home-cooked meals, quietly left on their doorstep (by arrangement) has been the 'help' most consistently valued by patients we have seen.

Be considered

Sometimes talking to someone with cancer is a bit like walking on eggshells. They are so sensitive and made so vulnerable by their diagnosis that the most innocent of remarks can be seen as hurtful, intrusive or unhelpful. I have had patients distressed and angry because someone told them they were 'looking well' and the person with cancer thought 'How dare they – they do not know what I am feeling inside.' Or patients distressed because someone said they were 'looking tired' – and they felt undermined by the person not recognising the huge improvement they had made. They felt they were looking better than they had for months. Or patients distressed because someone commented how their hair was growing back – when the patient had struggled for months to hide their hair loss using a wig – and now found that 'everyone' knew.

So perhaps the best suggestion is to revert to suggestion one – listen or ask questions (not many) and **be guided** by the patient as to where the conversation goes.

Be guided by the patient

Someone with cancer has had much of their autonomy 'robbed' from them – their time, their independence, what they eat, what they drink, their appearance, their hair. They often feel very vulnerable to external encounters. So, listen carefully to what they say when meeting them. If a question such as 'How are things?' causes them to veer sharply on to a discussion about the weather, follow them there – they do not want to talk about their health. This usually does not mean that they do not want to be greeted and acknowledged. I have had patients enormously hurt when they see neighbours or friends cross the road to avoid speaking to them. While I can understand that this is sometimes because the friends fear doing or saying the wrong thing, it is extremely difficult for the person dealing with cancer to consider that viewpoint. So be brave. Stop, listen, acknowledge – and if they want to move on, that is their right.

Be patient

This refers to patience in so many areas. Patience for the (undeserved) irritability, the (sometimes unreasonable) requests, the (apparent) lack of appreciation from someone who is too ill to acknowledge help. But patience is needed in other ways too. Often someone recovering is slow and unsure, taking much, much longer to complete tasks. The temptation to 'jump in' and do things on their behalf is huge – but can be very undermining for patients for whom the simplest of tasks can seem Herculean. So, even though it can be very difficult to watch someone who was an accomplished cook spend ten minutes peeling a carrot, watch, support, acknowledge, wait to be asked for help. Or ask, in a general way, 'Is there anything I can do to help?' rather than saying 'Will I peel that carrot for you?' and doing it in two minutes, further underscoring how far the person has moved from their baseline. You will be doing a huge amount in supporting them as they work to reclaim their lives

How to help when you are a parent of teenagers/young adults who have cancer

James was 18 years old when he was diagnosed with cancer. The only child of two devoted parents, he was aware that his diagnosis had rocked their world. His father, with James's permission, came to see me to discuss how they might manage. One of the most important messages that I wanted to give was that there is no 'one right way' to manage children. Most parents know their children better than anyone else. Being a parent of a teenager is challenging, even without a cancer diagnosis. It is a time when children are becoming adults, wanting to test the boundaries, express themselves, take on new challenges, develop outside the home. Being diagnosed with cancer can 'rob' teenagers of many of these opportunities. In James's case, the things he wanted to do – travel, experiment in new situations, engage in activities that were 'new' – became difficult, in some cases impossible. Yet he was determined that he would not allow cancer to 'rob him' of everything that he wanted in life. He was determined to continue his school exams; attend university; do a part-time job, even if his opportunities were significantly less. This meant that his anxious, worried, guilt-stricken parents had to stand by and allow him to experience his independence – spending long hours studying; attending lectures; doing exams; standing in a shop for hours in a day, serving customers in his part-time job – when they wanted to have him at home, wrap him in love and care and fiercely protect him from everything they could. For them, it was so difficult to allow him to do these things. Yet for James, these were the things that kept him going. Otherwise, he felt, he would have lost everything.

James's parents learned to sit and listen to him, and sometimes support him in decisions that they found difficult. He managed to sit his school exams, gain entrance to university and work his part-time job. It was not an easy balance.

It is extremely difficult being a parent to a young adult/ late teenager like James, who has cancer. Nowhere is the example of someone saying, 'I wish it were me, not them' more likely to be found. Teenagers and young adults with cancer particularly struggle with the resultant loss of independence, just at the time when they were trying to become independent in their lives. This means that as a parent you will be caught between wanting to help, perhaps needing to help, and yet having that help rejected and sometimes angrily rejected.

For you, all the suggestions already given are relevant. You will have to listen rather than speak, making clear that you hear and validate their opinion. You will need to be guided by the young person in front of you even when, sometimes, they are, in your opinion, making the wrong decision. They may need to learn from their mistakes (again, within reason – I am referring here to examples such as refusing to allow you to move their bed downstairs even when you know they would benefit, not refusing to attend hospital when they have an overwhelming infection). You will need to get as much help as possible from others in organising the practical things for home. And you will need to be kind to yourself (see below).

Often, parents of young adults feel they must be with, sit with their child/young adult, the patient, at all times because they are a parent, and it is their child, they feel responsible. This is not necessarily the case. Sometimes, the staff need an opportunity to form relationships and support this young adult/teenager who is ill. These relationships are often hugely helpful, and a key part of improving their lives. It cannot be done, or is extremely difficult to do, when someone else is sitting in the room at all times. Equally, many of these young adults may have difficult psychological issues they do not want to voice to their parents and will need an opportunity to speak in confidence with a team member. Sometimes, too, as part of a graded exercise regimen, for example, these young patients will have to be supported in testing themselves to their limits – something that is very difficult for a parent to watch. Finally, it is likely to be a long road – for you as well as the patient. So, you, the parent, will need to take a break, link with the rest of your family, recharge yourself, in order that you can continue to be the best support possible. So talk to them – listen to what they feel is helpful, and speak also to the staff to hear their advice.

How to manage your children when you, the parent, have cancer

Many patients with cancer will have young children – and what to say and how to manage are frequent questions. Much like the response to cancer, there is no single 'correct' way to manage and help your children if you have cancer. Every child, and every parent, is different, and every parent knows their children better than any health-care worker. It is, however, a myth to think that your children will not be aware that there is something 'going on'. They will quickly pick up on the stress and change of routine. It is always better to allow conversation, to hear their worries. If you have a partner, agree with them what you will say and, if possible, meet the children together. Be guided by the children, listen to what they ask. Give them some information, perhaps such as 'Mummy is sick at the moment and needs to go to hospital for treatment. She will be very tired some days so will need to rest.' And wait to see what they ask next. Or ask if they have any other questions.

It will, of course, depend on the age of the child. And you may need to meet some of your older children separately. A general rule, however, is that total concealment is neither a good idea, nor possible; and that telling the truth, within limits, is best, even if only some information is given. For example, 'Will you get better from this?' – an answer may be 'That is why I am going to the hospital to get treatment because I want to get better from it' – even if you are not absolutely sure yourself. If you are struggling to manage, or concerned about your children, then speak to your family doctor.

Be kind

I am sure you will be surprised to see this suggestion – affronted at the fact it is even included. I am sure you do not need to hear the suggestion to be kind to your loved one with cancer. But, in fact, this suggestion is to be kind to yourself. It is enormously difficult to be the onlooker to someone you love being ravaged by an illness and treatment. And, inevitably, the focus and support are on them and for them. And you may feel selfish, or even forget, to acknowledge your own distress and needs. Acknowledge it. Be kind to yourself. Get support for yourself. It is a hard road.

15

Cancer – Your Doctors Are Human Too

You may ask why on earth one would devote an entire chapter to the fact that your doctors are human too (and I am using the term 'doctor' as it reflects my experience, but you can substitute the term 'health-care professional' if you prefer). 'They are simply there to do their job,' I hear you say. 'Why should I care? I am the one with cancer.' That is, of course, true. You are the one with cancer, and you are the focus of care. And, generally, I say to you – you have enough to do managing your cancer without bothering or worrying about anyone else. Occasionally, however, I would suggest, as in, for example, the discussion on managing social interactions, that it is useful for you to consider others' perspectives as it may help you to better manage situations for yourself. Understanding the perspective from the other side will, I hope, allow you to better manage your own experience. It is in this context that I am writing about your cancer team and their representative doctors – to give you, and your families, some insight into the (possible) experiences of your teams because, as I constantly repeat, knowledge is power, and understanding their perspectives and experiences may help you to better understand your experiences and their reactions. There will be those of you who say – tough! I have enough on my plate. I cannot be thinking about them. And I agree. Your role is not to think about them to make them feel better. It is about thinking about them to help you. It is not necessary, but it may help. So, if you have the energy, read on. If not, open another chapter.

A cancer doctor's story – the impact of a cancer diagnosis

This story is **not** about a cancer doctor's own cancer diagnosis, but the impact on the cancer doctor of their patients' cancer diagnoses. And, while it is my own experience, you will see that it is the experience of many other health professionals too.

I recently met a cancer consultant with whom I had trained as a young doctor many decades previously. We were discussing the impact of working with cancer, and how patients continue to influence us, long after they have left our care. I told him about a chance recent meeting with a physiotherapist who, unknown to me, had also trained briefly on this consultant's cancer ward – 35 years previously – at the same time as me. We were discussing those early experiences and their impact. I had mentioned to this physiotherapist, without naming him, one person in particular, a young man, kind, gentle, uncomplaining, who had died of cancer in his mid-twenties. She immediately said she knew who I was referring to. I did not believe her – how could she remember from so long ago? But she not only described him perfectly, she remem-

bered his name. I was now telling my former colleague this story,
35 years after we had both looked after this patient. He immedi-
ately said, 'I know who you are talking about. It was a very sad
case. I can tell you his name, where he came from, his family
details.'

To those of you reading this book who have cancer, you may
say, 'That is hardly surprising – that is a very sad story.' That
is true. But all these health-care professionals look after tens,
hundreds, thousands of patients with cancer over a career.
And they remember the patients they look after, they leave
an impression. Why does this matter for you? Hopefully,
these experiences will make us better doctors, more empathic,
more understanding, better at managing the complex human
experiences that looking after patients with cancer bring. This
book is based on those lessons, on the strategies they have
taught us.

But life is not perfect, and doctors are human too. That is
why these events leave their mark. And that may influence
their interaction with you – for better or, hopefully rarely, for
worse.

The cost of managing a life 'outside' work

Most of us in medicine spend a long time in our training
focused on being 'professional' in our interactions with
patients, leaving our own problems at home, out of the interaction. This is appropriate and necessary – for many reasons.
Yet this is an almost impossible task. We are human too and

so will at times be tired, ill, distressed, overworked – but still be needed at work. We **should** be able to put that aside and focus solely on the patient in front of us. Generally, we can and do, but there will inevitably be some moments when the mask will slip and distress, tension, upset will be visible, even briefly. The difficulty for you, the patient, who, is, naturally, closely observing us for any possible sign that relates to yourself, is that you may interpret this as relating to you. You may not hear a single word of the consultation – remembering only the look of worry and tension on your doctor's face.

Dr Anne was an extremely hard-working, organised and capable cancer doctor, working full-time in a busy, challenging area of cancer care. She also had four children under the age of seven. We frequently stopped briefly during our rounds of the hospital wards to discuss the challenges of balancing a full-time career with school runs, after-school events, food shopping, meals, evening homework and night-time rituals. Despite the many demands on her time, she was always resolutely cheerful and I knew her patients valued her kind direct approach.

One Friday afternoon, we met on a set of stairs as we both did a 'final' round before the weekend. Sensing that she looked much less cheerful than usual, I wondered if she had had a difficult afternoon clinically and happened to stop to ask how she was. She told me instead about a whole range of problems that had suddenly arisen for her at home.

I totally understood Dr Anne's story, as would any parent involved in the tightrope-like effect of balancing home and work. She had always been wonderful at 'putting on a mask' in her clinical interactions. But I wondered if patients would sense the difference in her appearance and her manner on that day. I thought of 'Mary', my patient currently an in-patient under her care, who always watched every interaction with her doctors with minute attention to detail – and, driven by anxiety, invariably presumed it meant bad news about her cancer.

So the message from this example is – doctors are juggling complex lives too. The message is given not so that you can sympathise, empathise or feel their pain, but so that you can carefully protect yourself, recognise that the tense worried face may not be about your cancer, but may represent a 'leakage' from their personal face into their professional one – something we all fight against but occasionally we lose.

The cost of empathy

As doctors, we are, rightly, expected to be empathic – to 'feel our patients' pain', to 'put ourselves in your shoes' – as best we can; to listen, hear and see your point of view. We aim to do this repeatedly, throughout the day, every day, with the same degree of care and empathy for every patient. These experiences are part of the immense privilege of being a doctor. They give us the opportunity to truly engage in helping people's suffering and distress.

However, like all positives, there is a flip side. Working with cancer, these personal interactions can be extremely challenging. 'Pulling oneself together' to greet the next patient, leaving behind the last patient's distress, can truly be very difficult. We must be **empathic** but not **distressed, supportive** but not **controlling, honest** but not **blunt, objective** but not **callous**. This is a difficult task. To truly be empathic, one must fully engage with a patient's distress. To do this without becoming distressed is very difficult. Some doctors manage this well innately. Some find it impossible. Others manage by distancing themselves.

Jane, a young woman with breast cancer, referred to psycho-oncology, was sitting in my office, absolutely furious. She was so angry she could barely speak. Having had surgery in another country, she had moved back home for her chemotherapy. She spoke for 30 minutes without stopping, almost without drawing breath. None of her story related to her current problems. She was completely focused on an out-patient visit she had had with her cancer doctor abroad, six months previously. She described what she had said, then what the doctor had told her. Then she said to me, 'Silent tears began to roll down my face as he told me how bad things were. And do you know what he did then?' I shook my head mutely. 'HE KEPT RIGHT ON TALKING,' she shouted at me. 'HE NEVER EVEN STOPPED. HE NEVER SAID A WORD ABOUT MY TEARS. HE JUST KEPT TALKING AS THOUGH NOTHING HAD HAPPENED.'

I listened quietly. For Jane, this experience had been deeply traumatising. She described it as 'inhuman', the sense that the doctor in the room had not in any way noticed or acknowledged her distress. I acknowledged that it clearly had been a terrible experience for her, and one that was continuing to affect her many months later.

One of the difficulties in this story is the persistent impact this interaction had on this young woman. Distressed by her cancer diagnosis, her focus was on the apparent callousness and inhumanity of her cancer doctor. Her anger and distress about this, her sense of injustice and abandonment were impeding her ability to engage with her treatment.

Later, reflecting on the story, I wondered about other explanations. Whether, perhaps the doctor, himself traumatised after many interactions with difficult news, fearing being unable to manage her distress, had noticed her tears, but thought it better to keep going, in case she couldn't manage – or he couldn't? Was he 'blocking' his response? Because the opposite end of the spectrum is to experience the distress. And even the most seasoned of doctors, those well used to balancing this tightrope of empathy and distress, will, at times, be defeated.

Dr Jim was a very senior, capable cancer doctor, a good colleague of mine. We had both been working together on a very challenging case – a patient we had looked after together for many years, who was now dying.

One afternoon, I walked in to the patient's single room to see Dr Jim sitting quietly by the patient's bedside. The patient had slipped into unconsciousness. Dr Jim, his back to the door, had moved quickly to brush away the silent tears rolling down his cheeks. I had seen, but said nothing. Dr Jim mumbled a few words to me, stood up, squared his shoulders and strode out, down the corridor to continue his round. I watched him go, thinking of the number of patients who would meet him that day, unaware that the sadness in his eyes had nothing to do with their case, but were

211

caused by the impact of the slow death of a patient he had cared for over the previous 10 years.

The cost of honesty

Clearly, doctors must be honest. They must tell the truth. But again, as is echoed throughout the book, the manner in which they do this is key. In times past, doctors were seen as paternal figures – they 'knew best', they had the 'knowledge'. Doctors were often seen as arrogant, with patients having little or no input into decisions about their care. Now the pendulum has swung to the opposite point, supporting a concept that information and decisions should be shared and patients should be supported in coming to that view. This is generally 'a good thing'. However, sometimes the pendulum has swung too far. Everyone is seen as 'equal'. Conversations are 'shared'. While no one can argue with the concept of sharing conversations, it is, in my view, a dishonesty to our patients to say that everyone in the room is absolutely 'equal' with respect to cancer conversations. In the room is one person, shocked, distressed and ill with cancer, usually with no medical training, and another person who is well, does not have cancer, and has spent decades of training to become expert in the treatment of the cancer their patient has.

When teaching medical students about this concept of 'equality in conversations', I often use the example of my experience in taking my car to a mechanic for a service. I do not know anything about the workings of my car. I do not meet the mechanic and have a detailed conversation about the timer mechanisms and the sump gauge. I leave them the key, ask them if they can service the car, put right any problems and, ideally, not charge me any more than they did previously. We do not have an equal conversation. I do not expect one. It would not be possible. They have all the knowledge and expertise in this area. I have none. I have picked a highly recommended mechanic whom I trust, and I listen to their view.

Similarly, the conversation between a shocked, distressed person, ill with cancer, usually with no medical training, and another person who is well, does not have cancer and has spent decades of training in cancer treatment, cannot, in my opinion, be an equal exchange of views. It can be a **respectful, caring, supportive conversation**, where knowledge and guidance is given in that context. Yes, it is a difficult task – to be honest and collaborative but not paternalistic. It requires careful thought and consideration on the part of the doctor. Leaving a patient with 10 of the latest scientific articles on the role of adjuvant chemotherapy is not an 'equal' interaction. This usually makes the interaction more difficult for the doctor but that is their concern, not yours.

So for you, as the patient, do not be afraid to ask questions and ask for the answers to be adapted for you. You may also want to ask your doctor the question I discuss with many of my patients, 'What would you do, or what would you advise your sister/brother/son/daughter/parent to do in this situation?' And, when it comes to hearing what you think may be very difficult news – you have a choice. You can say, 'Tell me everything straight' or 'Tell me some of what may be happening but I do not want all hope to be taken from me' or 'I want my son/daughter/parent to be here and I may ask them to hear some of this without me.'

When treatment 'fails'

Some of the (many) rewards of working in medicine include the sense of 'making a difference', providing answers to patients in distress. These are also some of the hardest things to bear. Because with that sense of making a difference comes a huge sense of **responsibility** and an even bigger sense of **failure** when one doesn't have the answer.

Speaking at a palliative care conference some years ago, I listed the emotions experienced when cancer treatment fails – **distress, anger, fear, guilt, confusion, failure, sense of being overwhelmed.** Everyone presumed I was referring to the patient's response. The audience of cancer doctors became a little unsettled when I said that I was, in fact, talking about the responses I had witnessed in so many cancer doctors when cancer treatment 'fails'.

So, often it is not only the patient and the family who are struggling at the end of the road but also the doctors, who can find it very difficult to say, 'I can do no more to cure this cancer.' This is not to say that the doctor leaves their patient now. But it requires a different focus and one that does not come naturally to every doctor, particularly when the doctor has been key in the path to 'cure' the cancer.

The impact varies from doctor to doctor, and sometimes depends on the particular relationship they have with a patient – sometimes patients of a similar age, or of a similar age or background to their children, or similar background to their own, may particularly resonate with them in terms of distress when (active) treatment fails.

I had worked with Dr John for many years and knew him to be smart, capable and hard-working. He had referred many patients to me over the years. It was unusual for him to ask me to sit in on a family meeting. I knew the patient, a young woman he had looked after for many years. He had exhausted every single treatment option for her and now had to meet her distraught parents to give them the facts.

I watched and listened as he sat with the parents. As I listened and saw him grow more tense and ashen-faced as the conversation continued, I realised just how difficult it was for him. The patient was the same age as his own daughter and had gone to the same school. While he did not share that with the parents, I knew that it was making what was always a difficult situation even more difficult. He sat and listened to the parents' distress. At the end of the meeting, the parents left the room and Dr John caught my eye and shook his head. 'Not now,' he said. 'I have a whole ward of patients to see.' And, squaring his shoulders, he walked out of the room and on to the cancer ward, where many more patients were waiting for his personal input and expertise.

I do not know, but suspect Dr John did an excellent job of seeing all his patients that afternoon. I am sure that none suspected the distress he was feeling having said goodbye to a family he had looked after for almost 10 years. But, if any did pick up on a sad expression, a moment of uncertainty, this story is to say that it may not, in fact almost certainly did not, reflect their own case.

I have included a chapter on 'doctors (or health-care workers) are human too', not because I expect you, who are managing your own cancer, distress and difficulties, to manage theirs, or even to acknowledge theirs. That is neither your role nor your duty. It is merely that I hope it may help you, in managing your situation, to recognise that sometimes the 'sad look' or 'worried frown' has nothing to do with your case. It may instead be a 'leak', a brief slipping of your doctor's professional 'mask' – one that we all work hard to control, but can still happen at times. Because doctors are human too.

Section VI

CANCER AND DYING

16

Cancer and Dying

Without doubt, this has been the most difficult chapter in this book to write. Everyone working with cancer desperately wants their patient with cancer to survive, to live, to live well, and for the cancer to be 'gone' from their patient's life. Almost all our education and all our training is absolutely focused on this end point of 'treat and cure'. Trained for years to 'know the answers', most find it exceptionally difficult to call a halt to active treatment, to accept that nothing more can be done to eradicate the cruel disease. Many doctors (particularly cancer doctors) therefore find it extremely difficult to recognise and accept this. Yet dying is part of life, it is an inevitable end point for all of us, much as we all desperately strive to avoid considering, or even mentioning it. The difficulty is that it is the (almost unmentionable) reality for **some** of our patients with cancer that they will die **before they expected** and **before they wanted**, and we must find a way to help them with this. Titling this chapter 'Dying' is an acknowledgement of this fact.

If you are reading this chapter as a person with cancer, or family member of someone with cancer, who is at this stage of their illness, I recognise that this is an overwhelmingly difficult place to be. Having struggled through months, perhaps years, of gruelling, difficult cancer treatment, having endured the long climb of rehabilitation, having managed all those difficult social situations, having ridden the emotional roller-coaster of hearing the cancer was 'gone', getting the 'all-clear', it is indescribable to have one's hopes dashed, plunged back into the despair of more cancer and more treatment. If, however, this is where you are, then we need to examine that place and look to see if we can help in any way.

As always in this book, stories of our patients who have made this journey before you and have educated us in how they managed will be our guiding lights.

For patients

There is no right way – and no absolute certainty

John was a 62-year-old man with lung cancer, for whom there were no further 'active' treatment options. John and his wife both knew that his days were numbered and he was dying of the cancer. Fully informed, even though they both acknowledged this, they were both very clear, they wanted to continue with life as 'normally' as possible. As John said, he wanted to 'plan for the worst while hoping for the best'. He made his will, organised his affairs, but continued to plan for appointments over the following weeks and months. With the support of his local palliative care team, John lived for many more months than expected and, during that time, was involved with many family projects before ultimately deciding to be admitted to his local hospice for his final days.

Mia, a young married mother, with three children under six, had been diagnosed with a very aggressive form of cancer. She, with her husband, had several meetings with her cancer team. She absolutely refused to engage in any discussion about her prognosis, asking that her husband would speak on her behalf. Her husband was distraught but accepted her wishes. Mia had a very difficult treatment course and died in hospital without ever fully acknowledging what was happening.

John and Mia's stories represent the extreme ends of a range of responses. Most, almost all, of the patients I looked after, struck a delicate balance. While listening to news about prognosis and treatments and getting affairs in order, they rarely fully acknowledged that they were at the end of the road. They might recognise that things were difficult, they might stop asking about the future, but they generally continued to focus on getting through the next days, weeks or months. 'Never take away my hope' was the phrase one patient used, and one I never forgot.

Your doctors will often ask you 'What do you want to know?' or 'How much detail do you want?' If you can manage, it is usually helpful for you to hear, even once, and ideally with a family member present, what your situation is at present. You can continue to hope, always, for a new cure, or new possibilities. But, if you can 'plan for the worst while hoping for the best', as John said, that will be very helpful for family and loved ones. And perhaps, like John, even for yourself, the responsibility of worrying about everyone else will ease, allowing you to focus on yourself and your own care.

221

Catherine, a married mother of four children in their late teens, had reached the final stages of her cancer treatment. Her options had been exhausted and she knew she (probably) had a few months to live. She had attended the psycho-oncology service for several months early in her diagnosis for help in managing her cancer diagnosis and now re-attended for support in managing what were likely to be her final months.

She was particularly focused on her children and family, grieving the loss for them, and for herself. Having considered what she might do, she decided to create a 'memory box' for each child. This project engaged her for several months as she thought carefully about what would be most meaningful for each child, selecting photographs, treasured works of 'home-made' art, home-work copies, stories and notes. While she shed many tears in the process, when the time came when she was physically overwhelmed and too exhausted to continue, she felt she had 'done her best'.

Some people, like Catherine, like to gather records, letters, notes they want to leave – 'just in case'. These are very emotionally draining things to do, and, again, better to do with help. For some, they help to give a sense of control over what is happening.

Many others want to have as much certainty as possible about their care over the coming weeks and months. Make your wishes known. Do you want to go home? Do you want to be looked after in a palliative-care setting? Do you want to stay in the hospital? What symptoms or problems are most bothering you? What do you want your family to do? Do you want to speak to them or to have your team do that? Do you want to continue to be updated regularly, or would you prefer to nominate a loved one to be updated on your behalf? You still have choices about your care and your life.

For family and friends

Almost every patient has family and friends with them who are all also affected by their cancer diagnosis and yet are often unable to voice their own distress and concerns as they feel it is 'selfish' or they are not 'allowed' to be distressed, since they are not the ones with cancer. As discussed in the chapter on family and friends, supporting a loved one with cancer is distressing, tiring and, often, overwhelming. If you are now at this point of the journey where the person you have striven for seems to be reaching the end of the road, your challenges change. Furthermore, often the patient themselves is, at this point, so exhausted and worn out, that they are mainly preoccupied with managing themselves and their own needs on an hour-to-hour basis. You will be the ones 'still standing' who will need to manage this very difficult situation and support them to the best of your ability. This may be your last task on their behalf.

There is no 'right way'

As in all aspects of life, people are individuals, and everyone has their own style of interacting, relating and coping. It is the same with cancer and the same with dying. We all, therefore, clinicians and families, need to be guided by the individual within us, to **listen** to what they say.

Peter was a young man in his twenties, an in-patient in a cancer ward. He was dying from his cancer. His family, his friends and his cancer team were distraught. His team were particularly distressed as they felt Peter continued to act as if nothing was wrong – smiling, joking, making plans for his holidays. They felt, since he was so 'calm and cheerful', he could not possibly know what was happening and this was their fault for not making it clear. That caused them even more distress, so that they found it difficult to approach Peter to talk to him. They didn't know what to say.

They referred him to Psycho-oncology and asked me to see Peter. As I approached his bed, Peter said, 'I know who you are and why you are here. I know I am probably dying. I do not want to talk about it. Please ask everyone who is standing around my bed looking mournful to stop doing that. I do not want to focus on my death. I still hope something amazing will happen, that they will find something, a miracle cure. I am too young to die. I have spoken to my family, I have made my plans. If I need to talk any more, I will let you know. Now let me get on with what is left to me.'

Very many people are like Peter. At one level, they know they are dying; at another they do not want to accept it. They still want hope. And none of us have the right to take that hope away from them. Nonetheless, you as their family and we as their doctors must stand on this tightrope with them, doing a careful balancing act of supporting their hope, while also supporting them, practically and psychologically in the possibility that they have reached the end of the road. There will be some patients, like Mia, who never want to discuss the fact that they are dying. This is very difficult for families and friends, and particularly difficult in planning care. One must make sure that the patient has been told and is aware, and then one must step back and work around that as best as possible.

Most people, however, are willing to acknowledge it at some level – although often in different ways. Some will discuss it with health-care staff, but not with family. Others will acknowledge it, but will then also want to make plans for the next year, wanting to live with hope and willing to tolerate the ambivalence.

How to talk – how to listen

Joseph was an extremely kind, clever young man. Dignified, determined, kind-hearted, he had endured multiple gruelling rounds of cancer treatment, started in his early twenties. He had made multiple efforts to return to 'normal life' after each round. Now in his mid-thirties, I had been looking after him in the Psycho-oncology service during all those years – for brief periods at a time, but after 12 years, I knew him well.

Now he was succumbing to a cancer that was slowly overwhelming him. He knew. I knew. I knew he knew. But neither of us ever fully acknowledged it. He would sometimes ask me, a psychiatrist, how his cancer was doing – a question he knew I would not answer fully as I am a psychiatrist not a cancer doctor. I would sometimes ask him if he had asked his cancer doctor that question – but he would always 'dodge' it, saying they were 'too busy' or he 'forgot'.

Yet without ever directly voicing his wishes, he made very clear

225

what he wanted. He wanted to continue to attend the hospital where he had been looked after for 15 years of his adult life, to see the teams that he had known over that time. He wanted to continue to get support, pain relief and whatever other treatments were needed. He wanted to talk about 'normal' life, and he wanted, when it happened, to die at home with his family – his short time living away from home, starting his own career, had been cut short by another cancer relapse. At the time, he had quipped to me, 'I think I will always be a "renter" not an owner.'

He was always accompanied by his mother, a quiet gentle woman, who was steadfast in her support, but never intruded on his visits. She would drive him in, sit by his side and wait quietly outside the room until he was ready to go.

Over time, Joseph became too weak to walk into my clinic, so his mother pushed him in a wheelchair. Determined and proud as he was, I knew how much it cost him to be wheeled in this manner, but he never mentioned it and neither did I. At the end of every visit, I would give the option of when he would come back by simply asking him when he wanted to attend for the next appointment. He always booked the following week. I had learned, from so many others, to listen and respond. So, we would book his next visit for a week later.

I remember Joseph's last visit very well, even though it is now over 15 years ago. Joseph was wheeled in by his mother who, as always, quietly left to wait outside. He looked gaunt, weak, was speaking in a whisper. We had a brief discussion about his previous week and then he stopped, thanked me and said he would head back home. I went and brought his mother in so that she could wheel him out. As always, I paused and asked Joseph when he would like to come back. 'Next week, as always,' he whispered. I

*could barely look him in the eye as I nodded and made my note.
His mother silently wheeled him out. A moment later, there was
a knock at the door. Surprised, I went to answer it. His mother
stepped in, apologetically. 'Thank you for making the appointment,'
she said, 'but I do not think we will be here for the appointment
next week – I do not think Joseph will last that long.' I nodded
in agreement but said I would keep the time for him. I stepped
out into the corridor and watched as she quietly wheeled Joseph
down the long corridor of the out-patients, out through the door,
and turned left to leave the hospital.*

*I never saw Joseph again. Six days later, his mother phoned to
leave a message with my secretary to cancel Joseph's appointment
– he had died the previous day.*

The story of Joseph is a hugely important one. It was about
listening to what he wanted, being **guided** by him in the
conversation and in his needs, in what is such a difficult
journey – for everyone.

How to 'let go'

**It is extraordinarily difficult for relatives to allow a loved
one to die**, to 'leave'. This is particularly true for parents. It
is particularly cruel for parents to watch their children die
before them, even when those children are in their twenties
or thirties. It goes completely against the natural order of
life.

Many families have spent months, years, pushing, toiling,
striving, driving, doing everything in their power to keep their
loved one alive. They have sacrificed hours, months, years of

their lives doing this – often diverting their energy and care from themselves, sometimes other family members, and their own lives to do this. They have often literally 'willed' this person to live on. That determination and energy is what has kept them going through it all.

As a result, it can be so very, very difficult to acknowledge that the end of the road has been reached, that they have to let go. One family said it felt like they were loosening their own fingertips clasped on to their loved one, prising them off, one by one, fingertips clinging to a ledge. It is heart-breaking. And yet, if that is the stage of the journey, 'letting go' is what must be done. It is **not** 'prising off the fingertips'. It is allowing an exhausted worn-out person to lie down, be comfortable, be safe and be cared for. It is about enveloping that person in a warm, comfortable, sustaining, embrace as they breathe their last. Because for the patient, exhausted, worn-out, unable any more to continue the struggle to stay alive, that is the support they need. It is, however, for the family and loved ones, probably the most difficult task of all.

Isobel was in her mid-twenties. An amazing student, capable in both academic and sports fields, she had been diagnosed with a very aggressive cancer in her late teens. She was determined from the start to live a normal life despite this. And so began eight years of recurrent bouts of extremely difficult chemotherapy, radio-therapy and surgery. After each bout of treatment, she would struggle back to normal life, attending university, gaining not one, but two degrees. Even when not fully recovered, Isobel would be setting her next academic goal, working part-time to support herself (when she often could barely stand). This was a challenge for her cancer team, her psycho-oncology team and her family, who worried about the pressures she put herself under, but all accepted that this was 'Isobel's way' – she set herself targets and pushed herself to reach them. That was her way of coping.

Isobel's family were, unsurprisingly, like Isobel – capable, determined, supportive, focused on setting targets (mainly targets aimed at helping Isobel) and achieving them on her behalf – chasing down every possibly intervention, treatment options that might help.

Isobel's cancer came back four times. Each time, she became weaker, less able to recover. When her cancer came back for the fifth time, there were no active treatment options left. Her parents were devastated. Isobel herself was now so exhausted that she could barely lift her head from the pillow.

A wonderful person, very close to her parents, even in the midst of her own terrible situation Isobel thought of others, and particularly her parents. She knew how devastating it was for them. She wanted to keep going, 'to fight on, for them as well as for herself', but she could no longer do it. She was exhausted, weak, overtaken physically by her cancer. She needed to 'let go'. But she was also overwhelmed with guilt at the concept of 'laying down' her 'fight'. She found it difficult to even voice these thoughts.

One of my last conversations with Isobel was when she talked about how 'tired' she was, how she wanted to leave hospital, go home, be with her family, to 'have a rest'. Those were her words – and what she wanted me to say to her parents: she needed 'a rest'. She knew that the reality was that what she was saying meant stopping all searches for new experimental trials, no more optimistic conversations with her parents about 'new hope'. Without actually saying it, it would mark a complete change in her care. Now she needed warm support, to be wrapped in care, while she laid down her head and took her leave. She had done everything she could – now she was done.

I will never forget the family meeting with her parents. Her cancer doctor and lead cancer nurse were also struggling to accept the situation. I could see her parents' distress as they heard the frank discussion about their daughter's options. They would have to accept something that truly was almost unbearable to accept: that their determined, kind, witty, clever, beloved daughter, despite her incredible bravery, and their full, back-breaking support, was dying. They initially struggled in the conversation – 'What about option x, what about option y?' The cancer doctor repeated the reality, and Isobel's wishes: there were no active treatment options left, Isobel was exhausted, she wanted to go home – 'for a rest'.

I watched the light of hope die in her parents' eyes, saw the glance of communication between them as, even during the meeting, they began to gather themselves, to change their direction of support. Brave themselves, they now changed their focus to supporting their daughter in her final stages. Conversation became about which room in the house would be best for Isobel – the front room with a view of the garden, near to the kitchen; bringing her bed downstairs; arranging for the palliative care team to visit their home. They had begun the process of 'letting go'.

'Letting go' is, I think, the hardest challenge for any family (and team). Like everything, however, it is important to consider how one might do this. Firstly, one does need to be certain, or as certain as one can be, that this is, in fact, the stage that the person is at (speak to your cancer team). Secondly, it is not an 'all or nothing' approach. In fact, what is needed now from families and friends (and teams) is, often, more support than ever, being present despite huge distress, listening to your loved one's wishes; agreeing that, *for now*, any talk of 'overseas trips' for 'new high-intensity experimental treatments' will be put aside, if that is what the patient wishes. The difficulty for families is that, sometimes, the activity and energy spent in researching and organising new options has, until now, provided some distraction, some relief from the awful reality faced. Now, there are no distractions and they must sit and face what is for some an intolerable fate.

Isobel expressed this so well. She did not say, 'I am dying.' She said, 'I am tired and I want to go home.' And she **was** tired. She had spent 12 years determined to keep going 'no matter what' her cancer brought. But now had come the time when she could do it no more. And her heart-broken parents, who had striven, toiled and laboured to get her through so far, were suddenly faced with the fact that they could no longer focus on keeping her with them. They had to let her go. She was too exhausted to try anything else. And part of her worry now was the feeling she was letting her family down by 'lying down', by accepting that she could not go on any further.

So they had to tolerate this wall of grief, bring their daughter home. And ensure she had every support and comfort in her last days in their home. And they did. But it was a monumentally difficult task for them.

Palliative care

The palliative care team is a particularly key part of cancer care at this point. They may have been introduced earlier in care, relieving and managing pain and other symptoms. They are a vital part of 'end-of-life' care. They are comfortable in talking to patients (and families) about subjects such as death and end-of-life care, subjects that are often extremely difficult, for everyone, in the setting of acute high-intensity curative treatments.

Palliative care teams usually offer home-based and/or hospice care. You, and your family, can arrange with the team whether you would prefer mainly home-based or hospice-based care. A member of the team can call to your home to advise on symptoms and medications. They can provide (or help you to obtain) overnight cancer nursing at home, for example, often crucial for families who are exhausted and unable to manage their loved ones, particularly at night-time when people often become confused and distressed, and help seems difficult to access. Sometimes, either because symptoms cannot be managed at home, or the person wishes, they will arrange for admission to a local hospice, a centre specifically orientated towards symptom relief, care and, if appropriate, dying. Unlike hospitals, they can accommodate families and visitors throughout most stages of the admission, and have particular expertise – medical and social – in end-of-life care. I will reiterate what I have said previously. It is always worth-while to have met the palliative care team at an early stage of treatment, if appropriate. It is far better to have met the team and established relationships before (if) it becomes a necessary part of treatment. It also, usually, makes the transition to end-of-life care a less difficult process.

For those of you who have read through this chapter – the person with cancer, or the family or friend – I recognise it will have been a harrowing read. I earnestly hope that it is not a chapter that is relevant for you now. But I must echo what I said in the introduction. Everyone working with cancer desperately wants their patient with cancer to survive, to live, to live well and for the cancer to be 'gone' from their patient's life. Our patients, and their families, inevitably want the same. Yet dying is part of life, it is an inevitable end point for all of us, much as we all desperately strive to avoid considering or even mentioning it. And death **before they expected** and **before they wanted** is the (almost unmentionable) reality for **some** of our patients with cancer. We must find a way for us, and for you, to help them with this.

Epilogue

There are still many myths about cancer that drive people's fears. Thankfully, we now know that these are myths and that many people with cancer recover, and recover fully. Survival rates and treatments are improving all the time. There are many different types of cancer. Even in the 'same' area and now, even within the same cancer, people respond differently. One can never compare oneself to someone else's 'cancer story'.

This book has outlined the stories of people who, faced with a cancer diagnosis, found within themselves determination, resilience and hope, frequently beyond what they ever thought they had. For them, often the experience of being **heard and understood** was a powerful intervention. Practical support, providing meals, transport, support with children and family they also described as powerful interventions that are often not considered by distressed family and friends. More detailed expert interventions, describing and analysing fears, worries and struggles that cancer has brought to them can allow them to find solutions – empathically and objectively – to improve quality of life, support mental health and nurture wellbeing, both physical and mental. For most, the goal is to not merely resume one's previous life, but to resume the best life that one can.

Even in the most difficult of circumstances, there is a way forward.

Professor Anne-Marie O'Dwyer

Appendix

If you would like to read in further detail about some of the mental health strategies in this book, the following may be helpful:

Mind Over Mood: Change How You Feel By Changing The Way You Think

Dennis Greenberger, Christine Padesky

The Worry Cure: Stop Worrying and Start Living

Robert Leahy

Overcoming Insomnia and Sleep Problems: A Self-Help Guide Using Cognitive-Behavioural Techniques

Colin A Espie

Acknowledgements

As with any book, many individuals have contributed to this project, directly or indirectly – patients, colleagues, family and friends. The list is long, so I must thank you all collectively (and whole-heartedly), for your support, encouragement, enthusiasm, experience and wisdom, given generously to me during my decades as a doctor.

There is one colleague that I must name individually and that is Dr Sonya Collier (D. Clin Psych), Lead Clinical Psychologist, Psychological Medicine Service, St James's Hospital, Dublin, Ireland. Dr Collier worked with me for over two decades. When she joined the service, then in its infancy, as its first clinical psychologist, she ensured that clinical psychology was embedded within the service, working side by side with psychiatry and dedicated mental-health nursing, to make certain that patients received integrated medical and psychological care. Her teaching skills, professionalism and, above all, her clinical acumen, helped to shape the thinking and style of the Psycho-oncology service at St James's. We co-wrote several patient-education booklets and self-help guides for our patients at St James's, referenced in this text, developing unique clinical strategies, including a

Cancer-Related Fatigue Manual. She has since been joined by several other colleagues, who, following Sonya's lead, work together to ensure patients of the Psychological Medicine Service continue to receive a truly integrated biological and psychological approach to care.

About the Author

Professor Anne-Marie O'Dwyer is a clinical professor at Trinity College, Dublin, and a psychiatrist with almost four decades of clinical experience. She has worked at the Maudsley and Addenbrooke's Hospital and, more recently, at Trinity College and St James's Hospital in Dublin. O'Dwyer spent more than half of her career working directly with patients who have cancer. She wrote a textbook on psychological aspects of medical care for Oxford University Press. This is her first book designed for everyone.

Bedford Square Publishers

Bedford Square Publishers is an independent publisher of fiction and non-fiction, founded in 2022 in the historic streets of Bedford Square London and the sea mist shrouded green of Bedford Square Brighton.

Our goal is to discover irresistible stories and voices that illuminate our world.

We are passionate about connecting our authors to readers across the globe and our independence allows us to do this in original and nimble ways.

The team at Bedford Square Publishers has years of experience and we aim to use that knowledge and creative insight, alongside evolving technology, to reach the right readers for our books. From the ones who read a lot, to the ones who don't consider themselves readers, we aim to find those who will love our books and talk about them as much as we do.

We are hunting for vital new voices from all backgrounds – with books that take the reader to new places and transform perceptions of the world we live in.

Follow us on social media for the latest Bedford Square Publishers news.

🐦 @bedsqpublishers
🅕 facebook.com/bedfordsq.publishers/
📷 @bedfordsq.publishers

https://bedfordsquarepublishers.co.uk/